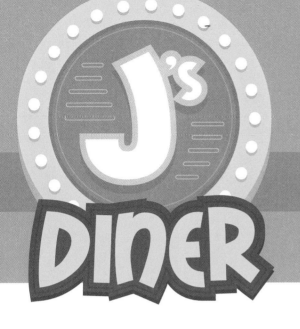

MENU

CHILDREN'S WORSHIP

PROGRAM GUIDE

JUMP CHILDREN'S WORSHIP

JUMP is a worship service intentionally designed to teach elementary aged children the importance of worship. During JUMP, children express their worship through high-energy music and dancing. The Bible lesson is further enforced through fun, engaging skits and object lessons. You will discover that JUMP is an exciting and engaging curriculum for children's worship!

VIDEO ELEMENTS

High quality video elements are incorporated to capture each child's imagination and to allow time for transition between live elements.

SKIT

With every lesson, a fun skit is performed to help put the main point of the day into a humorous, modern and memorable scenario. These skits are fun and serve as object lessons for the Bible story and main point. You and your kids will love laughing and learning with these fun characters. Children will not want to miss a single lesson!

On the skit pages, screen elements and AUDIO ELEMENTS are highlighted as cues for your audio/visual team.

Green text denotes important lines dealing with spiritual truths. Be sure your actors memorize the green lines!

MAIN POINT

The Bible is so rich! Every time we read a Bible story, be it the first or the fiftieth time, God can teach us something new. To help everyone stay on the same page, 28nineteen™ KIDS narrows in on one main point from the Bible story. Everything we do intentionally teaches the Bible story and this one point.

LEADER DEVOTION

The goal of the leader devotion is to help your leadership first learn the lesson personally which will help your leadership feel an empowerment and excitement to share what they have learned with their classes. For this reason, each lesson begins with the same devotion for all leaders on an adult level. Pertinent background information is incorporated to make the study richer in meaning for your leaders as well as for your kids.

JUMP BIBLE LESSON

JUMP Bible lessons are designed for large group teaching and often include object lessons and anecdotes to help teachers clearly present the Bible story and main point. Bible lessons are clearly outlined into three sections: Intro, Bible Story, and Application.

 Intro: Short for "introduction", this section helps leaders grab kids' attention, quickly review past lessons, teach the overarching theme of the series, and get kids excited about the Bible story.

 Read the Bible: Now, we get to the good stuff! In this section, leaders encourage kids to read in the Bible as they discover God's Word for themselves.

 Object Lesson: Object lessons use everyday, ordinary objects to teach important spiritual truths. A good object lesson helps the audience remember the spiritual truth in a tangible way.

 Application: Our goal is to teach children to be "doers of the Word, and not merely hearers" (James 1:22). To do this, we teach practical applications of Biblical truths in each lesson. The children should leave with a challenge or an action to live their lives for Christ.

JUMP TEAM

Often lessons refer to the JUMP Team. The JUMP Team is a group of highly committed, fun-loving volunteers. These upstanding high school volunteers and fun-loving adults lead worship by acting in skits, leading motions to songs, assisting with classroom management, interacting with children, and more.

ORDER OF SERVICE

Knowing each church has its own method of operating, JUMP curriculum is designed to be flexible. Each time segment in JUMP is clearly designated and can occur in whatever order you are most comfortable.

The following pages are an example of an order of service and are adaptable to any sized group.

JUMP CHILDREN'S WORSHIP
ORDER OF SERVICE

Pre-Service
This time before the service begins allows children to make it to their seats and interact with volunteers.

COUNTDOWN VIDEO

Song

MAIN POINT VIDEO

Welcome
The welcome is designed to introduce who is leading, what it means to worship, the rules for service, and what the children will learn that day. This should be done by the worship director, can involve a teacher/co-teacher scenario, and always ends with a prayer.

A few rules are said at the beginning of service so expectations for behavior are known. Always end with HAVE FUN!

Who's excited to be here today?! My name is (_____) and I am so happy you are here to worship with us! Today we are going to be learning that (MAIN POINT). Can you do those motions and say that with me on the count of three? One, two, three: (MAIN POINT). Oh, I think you can be louder than that! One, two, three: (MAIN POINT). WOW! Great job!

As you know, we come to JUMP to worship God together. What are some ways we can worship the Lord? We can worship God by singing, dancing, reading our Bible, and even praying! These are all ways that we worship God together. We are going to do ALL of those things today! We are going to learn some AMAZING things about God's Word, so everyone please sit up straight, look up here at me, and turn on your listening ears!

We have a few rules to help us worship God together. Rule number one is: (Stay quiet). When someone is speaking up here, please stay quiet. God has something to say to you and me today. We do not want to distract anyone from hearing exactly what the Lord has for us to hear.

Rule number two is: (Keep your hands and feet to yourself). We worship God when we focus on Him alone and put Him first. Keeping your hands and feet to yourself will help you and everyone around you focus on God.

Rule number three is: (Stand during songs). Anytime you hear a song, we stand so we can worship together, be reverent to the Lord, and show Him that we love Him. JUMP is a worship service, not a show. Stand up and participate with us when we worship through song!

Rule number four is: (HAVE FUN)! We are going to have so much fun today as we worship God together. Let's start this service right by talking to our amazing God in prayer right now.

PRAY

Song

SKIT INTRO VIDEO

JUMP Skit
The skit falls before the JUMP Bible Lesson, so the pastor or teacher can refer back to the lessons the characters learned during the skit.

GAME VIDEO

Song

BIBLE LESSON INTRO VIDEO

JUMP Bible Lesson

The Bible lesson falls roughly halfway through the service to make sure all of the kids have arrived. We do not want anyone to miss out on the best part! JUMP Bible lessons often include object lessons and anecdotes to help teachers clearly present the Bible story and main point in 15 minutes or less.

PRAY

We are about to go into our time of offering. "Offering" is a big word for present. This is the time when we give our presents to the Lord. We give back to God from everything He has given to us. Let's stand together and sing this song as an offering, a big present to God.

Offering Song

PRAY

MEMORY VERSE VIDEO

Memory Verse

The goal of the memory verse time is long-term understanding and memorization of Scripture. For this reason, 28nineteen Curriculum focuses on one verse or passage during each series. Throughout the series, kids are encouraged to memorize these verses by making motions to the words and repeating the verse together.

Song

Announcements

What can the children look forward to in your ministry? Use this time to encourage kids to bring friends and participate in whatever you may have coming up next.

Review Game

Play a fun game that allows everyone to remember what they have learned.

It's time for the REVIEW GAME! I need one volunteer from each grade to come up on stage. I want to choose people who have been listening and paying attention the whole service and want to play in our game!

During this game, your grade can win by getting very quiet when you hear the wrong answer and very loud when you hear the right answer. Each grade is going to have a different silly move and sound that you must do when you think you hear the right answer. *(Let your contestants choose a silly motion and sound for their grade.)*

I hope you are ready. I hope you have been paying attention. The game begins ... NOW!

(Ask review questions. Give kids the opportunity to do their motions and silly sounds when they hear the correct answer. Award points to the winning grade.)

Song

Dismissal

The PANTRY

OVERARCHING PLOT:

While Grandpa J is researching other diners across America, his grandkids, Pixel and Um, run J's Diner. Each day, they learn to follow Grandpa J's leadership. J's Diner becomes a popular restaurant once again.

MAIN CHARACTERS:

PIXEL - Tech savy, music loving, older brother of Um

UM - Talkative, story-telling, fun-loving, younger sister of Pixel

COSTUMES:

PIXEL - Orange shirt, jeans, white apron, and diner hat

UM - Purple shirt, jeans, white apron, and diner hat

SET:

"J's Diner", 50s themed diner with a few tables and chairs

LESSON 1

MAIN POINT The Lord Is My Shepherd.

SCRIPTURE Psalm 23:1; John 10:1-5

MEMORY VERSE Psalm 23

"**The Lord is my shepherd, I shall not want.**
He makes me lie down in green pastures;
He leads me beside quiet waters.
He restores my soul; He guides me in the paths of
righteousness for His name's sake.
Even though I walk through the valley of the shadow of death,
I fear no evil, for You are with me;
Your rod and Your staff, they comfort me.
You prepare a table before me in the presence of my enemies;
You have anointed my head with oil; My cup overflows.
Surely goodness and lovingkindness will follow me all the
days of my life, and I will dwell in the house of the Lord forever."

TODAY'S SPECIAL

PSALM 23:1

THE PANTRY

LESSON 1

OVERVIEW

SPIRITUAL CONNECTION:

Pixel and Um learn to obey Grandpa J, because he owns J's Diner. His instructions are meant for their good and for the good of the Diner. In Psalm 23, we learn to obey the Lord as a lamb obeys its shepherd. The Lord is our Shepherd, whose instructions are for our good.

CHARACTERS:

PIXEL - Tech savy, music loving, older brother of Um

UM - Talkative, story-telling, fun-loving, younger sister of Pixel

CUSTOMER - New customer to J's Diner

COSTUMES:

PIXEL - Orange shirt, jeans, white apron, and diner hat

UM - Purple shirt, jeans, white apron, and diner hat

CUSTOMER - Everyday attire

PROPS:

- White bread (Skit)
- Wheat bread (Skit)
- Salami (Skit)
- Ham (Skit)
- Pickles (Skit)
- Mayo (Skit)
- Cheese spread (Skit)
- Gummy worms (Skit)
- Tomatoes (Skit)
- Grape jelly (Skit)
- Button-down shirt (Bible Lesson)

LEADER DEVOTION • • • • •

PSALM 23:1 & JOHN 10:1-5.

For the next several lessons, we will be studying Psalm 23. Written by David, at one time a shepherd by trade, Psalm 23 reminds us there is great comfort in having the Lord as our Shepherd. The role of the shepherd is to provide, guide, protect, discipline, and generally care for the needs of the sheep. The role of the sheep is to simply follow the shepherd. This week, we will be studying exactly what it means to have the Lord as our Shepherd.

In Jesus' analogy in John 10, the Good Shepherd is the owner of His sheep, giving Him a more vested interest in their welfare. In fact, God owns us twice. First, He owned us because He made us. (Psalm 139; Genesis 1:26-27) God created us to live in a perfect relationship with Him. **However, as Isaiah 53:6 says, "All of us, like sheep, have strayed away. We have left God's paths to follow our own. Yet the Lord laid on him the sins of us all."**

When our sin separated us from God, Jesus came to pay the price for our wrongdoing with His death. He bought us back with His blood and became our Owner a second time. For those who have accepted His gift of forgiveness and restored relationship, Jesus is their owner not only once, but twice.

A shepherd has authority over his sheep. The sheep do not find a shepherd's authority oppressive, but comforting, because the shepherd cares for his sheep. A good shepherd has the flock's best interest in mind at all times. There is great rest in acknowledging God's authority over our lives. No matter how "out of control" a situation may feel in the moment, we can rest in knowing that God, our Owner who knows us each by name, is always completely and totally in control.

Imagine what would happen if a single sheep tried to control the flock on its own. It sounds ridiculous, but we do it all of the time. We try to take daily situations under our control and simply inform God of our progress. Ask yourself this question: Am I resting in God's ownership and authority over my life, or am I constantly fighting for control?

Pray over the kids in your group as you prepare. Ask the Lord to bring young hearts to Him. Acknowledge that He is in control and ask Him to work through you. Thank Him for being your Shepherd, your Owner, and your Authority.

LESSON 1

PRE-SERVICE

Play a combination of upbeat music and fun video elements before worship begins. Encourage your JUMP Team to welcome kids and engage them in conversation.

COUNTDOWN VIDEO

JUMP Worship is starting! Lead the congregation in counting down. Worshiping together is fun, and we are ready to begin!

SONG

Lead the congregation in a fun worship song.

MAIN POINT VIDEO

WELCOME

Welcome to JUMP, where we come to worship God together! My name is _____, and this is the JUMP Team. *(Introduce your volunteers.)* If you need anything during worship, let us know. We would love to help you. Today we start a brand new series called J's Diner. Have any of you ever been to a diner before? Me too! We are going to worship as we learn from fun skits, sing fun songs, and read from God's Word, the Bible.

Our main point today is "The Lord Is My Shepherd." *(Make motions for the main point. Have kids repeat the motions and main point with you.)* Shepherds are usually just for sheep. As we read from Psalm 23, we will learn we have a lot in common with sheep! I can't wait to learn more about what it means to have the Lord as our Shepherd.

To help us focus on God as we worship together, we have a few rules. The first rule is STAY QUIET. When someone is speaking, please stay quiet so you don't distract your neighbor from hearing exactly what the Lord has for us to hear. Rule number two is KEEP YOUR HANDS AND FEET TO YOURSELF. Focusing on God is very difficult when someone is poking you. Rule number three is STAND DURING SONGS. When you hear a song, we stand to worship together. JUMP is not a show! We want everyone to participate in worship with your heads, your hearts, and everything you have! Songs are a great time to stand and move as you worship God. The last rule is – say it with me - HAVE FUN! We are definitely going to have fun today at J's Diner!

Let's start worshiping God by talking to Him in prayer. Everyone bow your heads and close your eyes. We bow our heads out of respect to God, and we close our eyes to help us focus on God alone.

PRAY

Lead the congregation in prayer.

SONG

Lead the congregation in a fun worship song.

JUMP SKIT

See skit script beginning on page 14.

THE LORD IS MY SHEPHERD

LESSON 1 SKIT
THE LORD IS MY SHEPHERD

PIXEL enters.

PIXEL: Hurry up, Um! You're going to be late for our first day of work here at Grandpa's diner!

SFX: CRASH

UM: Ouch!

UM enters.

UM: Um, sorry, Pixel. I can't believe it! My first real job!!! And I know just how to start. Grandpa J is always telling us to be on time, prepared, and friendly.

PIXEL: Well, you're definitely not on time ...

UM: That's true ... But at least I'm prepared, and I've got my apron!

PIXEL: Where is it?

UM: *Looks down.* Aw man ... I got this! *When UM cannot find the apron, UM makes a paper towel bib. In the process, UM accidentally hits PIXEL in the face.*

SFX: SMACK

PIXEL: You hit me in the face!

UM: So be on time, be prepared and ... oh be friendly!!! I'm gonna introduce myself to all our customers! *Looks around and sees no one sitting at the barstools.* Where is everybody?

PIXEL: That's the problem. Grandpa J asked us to help get the word out about the diner. Not enough people are coming. We only have seven days to get this place back on its feet. If we don't get customers back here at J's Diner, then we'll have to close the diner down.

UM: CLOSE THE DINER?!? **SFX: DUN DUN DUN** Oh no!! We better get busy and find some customers!! *Starts to run away, PIXEL grabs UM by the sleeve.*

PIXEL: First, let's get some direction from Grandpa J! He said he'd be checking in with us on the computer while he's out of town to make sure things go smoothly while we're here. Grandpa J, are you there?

Grandpa J Video 1

> **GRANDPA J:** Hello? Is this thing on? Eh, I don't think it's on ... *Fiddles with the computer, getting close to the camera.*

PIXEL: We're here, Grandpa J! We can hear you just fine!

> **GRANDPA J:** Oh! There you are! Hey hey hey!! It's a great day with Grandpa J! I'm so excited you two made it down there today to help me out. I'm just sad I can't be there with ya. I'm out touring the country's best diners so I can get some new fresh ideas for J's Diner! I'll be back soon though and we can celebrate all of your hard work then. I sure hope you two can help me get my store back on its feet. Now remember, whenever a customer walks through the front door, you must do J's Jivin' Jingle. It's the way we greet all our customers!

PIXEL: I love J's Jivin' Jingle!

> **GRANDPA J:** Great! Now, the first thing I was thinking you two could help me come up with is a brand new sandwich for my menu. I think a new sandwich might be just what we need to get the diner back up on its feet! I know you will come up with something great! Just remember to include the family's secret ingredient. If it doesn't have the secret ingredient, I can't put it on the menu, okay? Bye kids! I know you will do a great job!

PIXEL & UM: Bye, Grandpa!

Grandpa J Video 1 ends

PIXEL: *Aside - PIXEL doesn't acknowledge UM trying to stop him.* Secret ingredient? I think I can come up with my own special super secret ingredient.

UM: Ummm ... Pixel, Grandpa J said to use the FAMILY'S secret ingredient.

PIXEL: Then, we'll have two secret ingredients for the diner!

UM: But Pixel ... Ummm ...

PIXEL: Of course, MINE will be the one that everyone will love.

UM: EARTH TO PIXEL!!! I really think we should just do what Grandpa J said and use the family's secret ingredient.

PIXEL: But mine's gonna be better! And anyway, my sandwich will be the best sandwich the world has ever known!

UM: Ummm ... No, if anybody's sandwich is gonna be better, it's mine! My sandwich will blow the taste buds right off of your tongue with its awesomeness!!!

PIXEL: Prove it.

UM: You're on.

SFX: FUNNY MUSIC

PIXEL and UM start to build their sandwiches, calling out the ingredients in a competitive way. As they build the sandwiches, they stop thinking about the contents of their sandwich and start thinking about having more unique ingredients than the other person.

PIXEL: White bread!

UM: Wheat bread!!!

PIXEL: Salome!!

UM: Ham!

PIXEL: Pickles! You've just been pixelated!!!

UM: Oh yeah?? Tomatoes!

PIXEL: Mayooooo!

UM: Cheese spread!

PIXEL: Starting to get worried, fumbles around for another ingredient. Grape jelly!

UM: OOOOh yeah??? More cheese spread!!

PIXEL: OOOOh YEAHHH??? Gummy worms!

UM: OOOOh YEAHHH??? More CHEESE SPREAD!!!!!! Beat that, Pixel!

CUSTOMER enters.

SFX: DOOR CHIME

UM and PIXEL freeze, look at each other, the customer, then back at each other.

SFX: J'S DINER JINGLE

CUSTOMER sits. PIXEL and UM run around the bar with their sandwiches, out of breath; trying to talk over each other.

UM: Um, hello. Welcome to J's Diner. My name is Um.

PIXEL: Would you like to try our new menu item?

CUSTOMER: Well, what is it?

UM: It's our new sandwich, and it's called Um's Ultimate Ummy Sandwich.

PIXEL: No. It's called Pixel's Perfect Panini.

PIXEL & UM: It's an explosion of flavor in your mouth!

PIXEL and UM try to get the customer to try their sandwiches. CUSTOMER smells them.

CUSTOMER: Woah! Those smell …

UM: They smell great, right? My sandwich will blow the taste buds right off your tongue with its awesomeness!!

CUSTOMER: Ummm …

UM: Yes?

CUSTOMER: I believe you … You know what I just remembered? I left the iron on at my house, because I was going to iron a sweater for my pet dog … Pickle …

PIXEL: Your dog's name is Pixel?

CUSTOMER: No - Pickle … Anyway, if I don't hurry to put her sweater on, she might catch a cold … and I uhh … Gotta go!

CUSTOMER runs out.

UM: Look what you did! We're supposed to be getting more costumers to WANT to come here so the diner doesn't have to shut down ... but now that customer is never coming back here!

PIXEL: No. They ran out of here because of your stinky sandwich!

UM: My stinky sandwich?!?! No one would EVER eat YOUR stinky sandwich!!!

SFX: VIDEO CHAT RING

PIXEL & UM: Oh no ... Grandpa J is calling!!

They hide behind the counter until they finally know they have to face him and slowly come out from hiding in shame.

Grandpa J Video 2

> **GRANDPA J:** Well, hey hey hey! It's a great day with Grandpa J! Hello? Hello?? Pixel? Um? Are you there? I just wanted to check in to see how the new lunch item was coming along ... It looks like you two have made quite a mess there. Did you include my secret ingredient?

PIXEL & UM: ... Oops ... Um, No, we didn't.

> **GRANDPA J:** I told you two that if it doesn't have the secret ingredient, it can't be one of the new menu items. Don't forget, I am your Grandpa, but I'm also the owner of J's Diner. The menu items have to be approved by me. I wanted you to come up with something great, but you have to do what I say if you're going to work for me, okay kids? I'm only looking out for the best for you two.

PIXEL & UM: We understand.

> **GRANDPA J:** Don't you know kiddos, just like I am looking out for you, the Lord looks out for all of us! He is our Shepherd. Maybe it would help you remember that if you say it with me. Can you do that for your silly old Grandpa, Pixel and Um? Say, "The Lord Is My Shepherd" all together now!

PIXEL & UM: The Lord Is My Shepherd.
> **GRANDPA J:** Great! Now, we'll have a fresh start tomorrow, okay?

UM: Okay. Sorry about the mess.

PIXEL: We'll get it all cleaned up and work on our new menu item with the FAMILY secret ingredient.

PIXEL & UM: Bye, Grandpa J.

Grandpa J Video 2 ends

PIXEL: Man, I feel really bad. We should have done what Grandpa J said. He is the owner, which means he's in charge.

UM: Yeah. And I guess my Ultimate Sandwich wasn't so ... Ummy.

PIXEL: And maybe mine's not so perfect. Technically, it wasn't even a Panini. If we're going to get this store back on its feet, we need to listen to Grandpa J. He knows what's best for us and for the store. Um, will you help me make a new menu item? This time maybe we can work together?

UM: I'll go get the secret ingredient. Oh, and by the way, I'm sorry I made fun of your sandwich. I'm sure it's delicious.

PIXEL: You could try it.

UM: Only if you want to try a bite of mine. It's gonna blow your taste buds right off your tongue ...

PIXEL: With awesomeness, right? Okay, deal.

UM: I have an idea! Let's combine our sandwich and make the UMMY PANINI SECRET INGREDIENT SANDWICH!

PIXEL: THE UMMY PANINI SECRET INGREDIENT SANDWICH? THAT'S GENIUS!!!

SFX: DINER EXIT MUSIC *PIXEL and UM try each other's sandwiches. Exit gagging.*

GAME VIDEO

SONG *Lead the congregation in a fun worship song.*

BIBLE LESSON

BIBLE LESSON INTRO VIDEO

 INTRO

Read Psalm 23 together.

For the next few lessons, we are going to study one chapter in the Bible, Psalm 23. The book of Psalms is in the Old Testament near the middle of your Bible. Psalm 23 was written by David. David grew up as a shepherd boy but later became one of the greatest kings of Israel. Psalm 23 is a song that compares the relationship of sheep and a good shepherd to a Christian's relationship with God.

 ## READ THE BIBLE

Psalm 23:1 says, "The Lord is my shepherd. I shall not want."

The shepherd in Psalm 23 owns his sheep. Shepherds are in charge of taking good care of the sheep. If you were a sheep, you would want to have a very good shepherd to take care of you!

In John 10:11, Jesus tells us, "I am the good shepherd; the good shepherd lays down his life for the sheep."

Again in John 10:14, Jesus says, "I am the good shepherd, and I know my own and my own know me."

Jesus calls Himself the Good Shepherd. That means Jesus loves you and wants to take care of you. He wants to be in charge of your life, so He can lead you in the right way and give you a home in Heaven. But Jesus doesn't force us to be His sheep. He gives us a choice. When we choose to make Jesus the Shepherd of our lives, it means that we choose to stop living our way and start living for Jesus.

Picture this:

When a shepherd first gets his sheep, he makes a mark on the sheep's ear to show his ownership. It's the same idea as branding cattle. This is a painful process, but one that must be done. A good shepherd puts his mark on the sheep, so everyone will know that the sheep belong to him and no one else.

In the same way, it can be painful to give up our lives to Jesus. Even though we know Jesus is the Good Shepherd, we are often tempted to try living life our own way.

 # OBJECT LESSON

Why should we obey Jesus, the Good Shepherd? Think about it like this: There is a right way and a wrong way to button this shirt.

(Hold up the button down shirt. Put it on without buttoning it up.)

- What is the right way to button this shirt?
- What would happen if I decided to do it my own way?

(Begin to button the shirt in the wrong way, overlapping buttons and twisting the shirt front until all the buttons are connected and the shirt looks messy.)

My shirt is all messed up! I should have started out buttoning my shirt the right way. Even choosing to do one button the wrong way made my shirt look messy.

(Unbutton the shirt and set it aside.)

In the same way, God knows the right way for us to live. We should choose to follow Him and His instructions, because He knows how to take care of us. God made us and loves us very much.

 # APPLICATION

In each lesson, we will have a road sign to help us remember what we learned from Psalm 23. Today, we learned to YIELD to God's authority and ownership over our lives. On the road, a yield sign means that you have to give up your right to go first. You have to let other cars go before you. Today, this sign is going to remind us that we should give up doing things our way and do things God's way instead. When we YIELD to God's authority, choosing to live His way, we choose to make God the Shepherd of our lives.

That is a very good thing!!

Choosing to make Jesus the Shepherd, the Boss, of your life is the most important decision you can make. We all need Jesus, because all of us have sinned at some point in our lives. We have all chosen to do something wrong. Those wrong choices separate us from God. Jesus, the Good Shepherd, came to earth and took the punishment for our sins, so we could become His sheep. Now, we can belong to Him and start a relationship with God as our Shepherd.

If you have already chosen to make Jesus the Boss of your life, you can be excited that Jesus is your Good Shepherd! Yielding to God's authority is exciting, because we are cared for by the greatest Shepherd there ever was or will be. We have Jesus as our Good Shepherd! We can be thankful that God loves us and takes care of us as His own children.

"The Lord is my shepherd. I shall not want." (Psalm 23:1)

PRAY

We are now going into our time of offering. "Offering" is a big word for present. This is the time when we give our presents to the Lord, our Shepherd. We give back to God from everything He has given to us. Let's stand together and sing this song as an offering, a big present to God.

OFFERING SONG

Lead the congregation in a slower worship song.

PRAY

Lead the congregation in prayer.

MEMORY VERSE VIDEO

MEMORY VERSE

Everybody stand up and stretch, because we are going to memorize all of Psalm 23! Don't worry. We are not going to memorize the whole chapter today – just the first verse. Memorizing can be hard, but I know you are all smart enough to memorize the whole chapter by the time we finish our J's Diner series.

The first verse says, "The Lord is my shepherd, I shall not want." As we just learned in our Bible lesson, this verse reminds us Jesus is the Good Shepherd. He gives us everything we need to do what He has told us to do. *(Make motions for the key words in the verse. Use the motions each time you say the verse.)*

Psalms is a book of songs, and Psalm 23 is a song King David wrote to the Lord. Since it is a song, I am going to sing the word "Psalm."

Repeat after me: Psaaaaalm 23:1 *(Psaaaaalm 23:1)*
The Lord *(The Lord)*
is my *(is my)*
shepherd *(shepherd)*,
I shall not *(I shall not)*
want *(want)*.

Good job! Now repeat a little more this time.
The Lord is my shepherd. *(The Lord is my shepherd.)*
I shall not want. *(I shall not want.)*

Great! Now say the verse with me on the count of three. One, two, three: "Psaaaalm 23:1 The Lord is my shepherd, I shall not want."

Can you say this without looking at the screens? Memorizing is hard, so take a second to shake it out. *(Take the verse off the screens as you say the verse together one more time.)*

Okay here we go! One, two, three: "Psaaaalm 23:1 The Lord is my shepherd, I shall not want."

Amazing! I can't wait to hear all of you saying all of Psalm 23 from memory. You are so smart!

SONG

Lead the congregation in a fun worship song.

ANNOUNCEMENTS

Use this time to encourage kids to bring friends and participate in whatever you may have coming up next.

REVIEW GAME

It's time for the REVIEW GAME!! I need one volunteer from each grade to come up on stage. I will choose people who have been listening and paying attention the whole service and want to play in our game.

Choose contestants and introduce them to the group in game show style.

During this game, your grade can win by getting very quiet when you hear the wrong answer and very loud when you hear the right answer. Each grade is going to have a different silly move and sound that you must do when you think you hear the right answer. *(Let your contestants choose a silly motion and sound for their grade.)* I hope you are ready. I hope you have been paying attention, because the game begins ... NOW!

Give kids the opportunity to do their motions and silly sounds when they hear the correct answer. Award points to the grade who is the quietest when they hear the wrong answer and participates the most when they hear the right answer.

Question 1: Our main point today is "The _____ Is My Shepherd."
    a. Pizza Guy   **c. Lord**
    b. TV   d. Cute baby goat

Option: Find a short video clip of a baby goat screaming online. Play this short clip every time you use "baby goat" as a choice. Act surprised and confused every time it plays. Let the kids laugh, then repeat the question again.

Question 2: Where can you find today's Bible lesson?
    a. Genesis 23   **c. Psalm 23**
    b. Hymn 23   d. Proverbs 23

Question 3: Who wrote Psalm 23?
    a. David   c. Peter
    b. Jonathon   d. A baby goat

Question 4: Psalm 23:1 says, "The Lord is my Shepherd. I shall not _____."
    a. ... forget this verse.   **c. ... want.**
    b. ... panic.   d. ... eat donuts.

Question 5: Who is the Good Shepherd in John 10?
    a. Jesus   c. David
    b. Your dad   d. A baby goat

Question 6: Name two ways Jesus is like a good shepherd.

SONG

Lead the congregation in a fun worship song.

DISMISSAL

J's DINER

LESSON 2

MAIN POINT The Lord is My Provider.

SCRIPTURE Psalm 23:2; Matthew 6:25-34

MEMORY VERSE Psalm 23

"The Lord is my shepherd, I shall not want.
He makes me lie down in green pastures;
He leads me beside quiet waters.
He restores my soul; He guides me in the paths of
righteousness for His name's sake.
Even though I walk through the valley of the shadow of death,
I fear no evil, for You are with me;
Your rod and Your staff, they comfort me.
You prepare a table before me in the presence of my enemies;
You have anointed my head with oil; My cup overflows.
Surely goodness and lovingkindness will follow me all the
days of my life, and I will dwell in the house of the Lord forever."

TODAY'S SPECIAL

PSALM 23:2

THE PANTRY

LESSON 2

OVERVIEW

SPIRITUAL CONNECTION:

Pixel and Um waste a lot of energy worrying. Instead of using Grandpa J's provisions, they try creating a party atmosphere on their own. Ultimately, Pixel and Um learn to trust Grandpa J, because he already provided everything they needed. In Psalm 23, we learn the Lord always provides everything we need to do what He has called us to do. We never need to worry.

CHARACTERS:

PIXEL - Tech savy, music loving, older brother of Um

UM - Talkative, story-telling, fun-loving, younger sister of Pixel

COSTUMES:

PIXEL - Orange shirt, jeans, white apron, and diner hat

UM - Purple shirt, jeans, white apron, and diner hat

PROPS:

- Spinny sign with sandwich name on it (Skit)
- Rubber chicken (Skit)
- Maracas (Skit)
- Top hat (Skit)
- Sunglasses (Skit)
- Baseball bat (Bible Lesson)

LEADER DEVOTION ● ● ● ● ●

PSALM 23:2 & MATTHEW 6:25-34.

When a sheep is discontent, it cannot rest. If the sheep is fearful, hungry, bothered by pests, or bothered by other sheep, it simply cannot lie down to rest. Interestingly enough, the solution to all the sheep's problems is the shepherd. Sheep have no means of protection except their instinct to run. A shepherd must protect his sheep from wild animals or thieves. Sheep cannot make the grass grow. The shepherd has to work the ground to make the fields green for the sheep, which is no small task in the dry and arid climate of Bethlehem. Sheep cannot eliminate pests. Shepherds must keep a watchful eye on their flock to make sure they catch and treat pest problems early. Finally, sheep keep a natural order called "the butting order." Older sheep butt the younger ones to let them know who is in charge of the flock. When the shepherd is present, this is much less likely to happen, as the shepherd is clearly in charge.

In every situation, the shepherd is the key to the sheep's contentment. In the same way, we can be content, because the Lord is our ever-present Shepherd. He takes care of our every need. There is no need to fear for protection, hunger, conflicts with others, or any other bothersome life situation when He is near. The key to contentment is the direction of our focus. Replace the worry with a focus on the things of God and His Kingdom.

Where is your focus? Are you focused on the things that worry you or are you focused on your Shepherd who makes you able to lie down and rest? It is easier to focus on the problems that face us each day, especially when they seem to surround us. But even sheep have to look up to see their shepherd. Take the challenge this week to examine the areas of your life where you are discontent. Examine the causes of your discontent and determine to give control over those areas to the Lord. Look up to Him, as He is the only One who can provide rest.

Pray over the kids in your group. Ask the Lord to give them rest from the worries they face at home or at school. Pray that God will use you to remind them that He is their Shepherd. He will take care of everything they need, just as He takes care of everything you need. Thank Him for leading you to areas of spiritual rest and fullness. Thank Him for being enough.

LESSON 2

PRE-SERVICE

Play a combination of upbeat music and fun video elements before worship begins. Encourage your JUMP Team to welcome kids and engage them in conversation.

COUNTDOWN VIDEO

JUMP Worship is starting! Lead the congregation in counting down. Worshiping together is fun, and we are ready to begin!

SONG

Lead the congregation in a fun worship song.

MAIN POINT VIDEO

WELCOME

Welcome to JUMP, where we worship God together! As you can see, we are in J's Diner, a fun, fifties style restaurant. We are going to watch funny skits in the diner, sing songs, learn from God's Word, the Bible, and even play games. Everything we do in JUMP is worship when we are fully focused on putting God first.

Today our main point is "The Lord Is My Provider." A provider is someone who gives you what you need. For example, your parents provide food, shelter, and clothing for you. They take care of you. Psalm 23 teaches us the Lord is our Provider. (*Make motions to help kids understand the Main Point. Repeat the Main Point a few times together before continuing.*)

To help us stay focused on the Lord, we have a few rules. Rule number one is STAY QUIET. God has something He wants to say to you today, and we do not want you to miss it! When we learn our Bible lesson, sit up straight and pay attention with your head and your heart. Rule number two is KEEP YOUR HANDS AND FEET TO YOURSELF. Focusing on God is very difficult when someone is poking you. Do not distract the people around you from worshiping God! Rule number three is STAND DURING SONGS. When you hear a song, we stand to worship together. JUMP is not a show! We want everyone to participate in worship with your heads, your hearts, and everything you have! The last rule is – say it with me – HAVE FUN! We are definitely going to have fun today at J's Diner!

Let's start worshiping God by talking to Him in prayer. Everyone bow your heads and close your eyes. We bow our heads out of respect to God, and we close our eyes to help us focus on God alone.

PRAY

Lead the congregation in prayer.

SONG

Lead the congregation in a fun worship song.

JUMP SKIT

See skit script beginning on page 32.

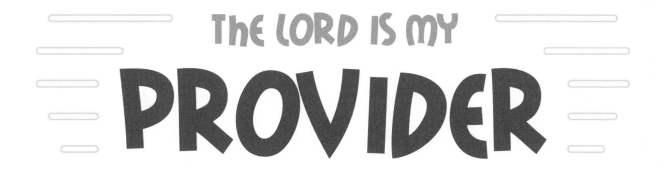

THE LORD IS MY
PROVIDER

LESSON 2 SKIT
THE LORD IS MY PROVIDER

SFX: INTRO MUSIC

PIXEL: I am so excited about our second day of work here at Grandpa J's Diner!

UM: I know Pixel! This is UMMM AWESOME!!

SFX: J'S DINER JINGLE

PIXEL: Now that we've added Grandpa J's Secret ingredient to our sandwich, I really hope we can really help get this store back on its feet, and get customers here again so the diner doesn't have to shut down! I know Grandpa would be so sad if we had to shut the doors to the diner because there wasn't enough business.

UM: If the diner shuts down, I don't know how I could go on! Where would we go for food? Where would we spend our summers? Where would we eat the best sandwich EVER?! *Shaking PIXEL in a panic.* DON'T LET IT HAPPEN TO ME, PIXEL!! *Accidentally hits Pixel in the face.*

SFX: SMACK

PIXEL: You hit me in the face! Um! You gotta calm down! Grandpa said he would help us out and provide everything we would need to get this diner hopping and happenin' again!

Grandpa J Video 1

> **GRANDPA J:** Well, hey hey hey! It's a great day with Grandpa J! Thanks for all your hard work yesterday at your first day of work! I really believe you two have what it takes to get this diner up and going! Now, today ... I have a big task for you two! Think you can handle this task?

UM: I CAN HANDLE ANY TASK!!!

PIXEL: So can I! I am older than Um anyway, so that means I'm a lot smarter and better looking, obviously.

GRANDPA J: Okay, okay, I know you're excited. But here's what I need you to do. I want you two to host a party for our customers to attend! I really think a party will help get our customers back to the diner and excited to see the new sandwich you two came up with yesterday!

PIXEL & UM: You mean the ... UMMY PANINI SECRET INGREDIENT SANDWICH?

GRANDPA J: Yes. That's the one! We want everyone to come out and try it at the party! Pixel, since you're good with computers, I'd like you to get online and advertise about the party. Get on those social media things you kids are on these days. Get on your bookface, tweeter and telegram and make sure everyone knows about the party at the Diner tonight! Um, I need you to set up for the party! *GRANDPA J rambles about party and how he has provided supplies in the warehouse. There's a box with paper, plates, balloons and streamers! Everything you need, ETC.*

UM: A PARTY?!?!?! I love parties!! *Excessive celebration and not hearing Grandpa J's dialogue about the party.*

Grandpa J Video 1 ends

UM: This is the best task ever! A party! We have to make it the GREATEST PARTY EVER!! Grandpa needs us, Pixel! This is it!! This is our time to shine!!! *UM doesn't listen to anything Pixel is saying.*

PIXEL: You're right Um! This is an important task and we need to get busy! We only have a little while until the party begins. I've got to get busy telling people about the party! You get ready to set up! Let me know if you need anything. Remember, Grandpa has provided everything you need.

PIXEL exits.

UM: *Becoming Very Stressed/Anxious.* Wait! I hope I can take care of it all. I don't want the diner to go out of business ... *Reluctantly.* I can do this. You can do this, Um! I can get this party put together all by myself! Um ... Oh, I know! We need to have a gigantic cake made of chocolate pudding!! Then we can have caramel covered apples. No, no, no - caramel covered spaghetti! I love spaghetti!!! We need squirrels! Maybe we could have dancing squirrels wearing their pajamas! Now that'd be a party! Ohhh, and we need A SPINNY SIGN! Yes! That's it! I'm brilliant! We need to stand outside the store and hold a sign to spin around, so people will know we are HERE! COME TO J'S DINER! Try our UMMY PANINI SECRET INGREDIENT SANDWICH! And I'll spin the sign like this, and this, and this, and watch out!! Customers will be lined up out the door! *Does ridiculous moves while spinning imaginary sign.* I've gotta get started!
UM exits.

UM comes back on with spinny sign and a bag of random items.
UM: I GOT IT! Here it is. A spinny sign!!! However, I did have a difficult time requesting dancing squirrels this time of year! Now, I must practice my spinning … here we go!

SFX: J'S JIVIN' JINGLE *UM tries to sing the jingle while spinning sign.*

PIXEL walks on and sees UM.

PIXEL: Um, what are you doing? The party starts really soon! I've had tons of people send me messages to let me know they'll be here! Where are all the plates, the streamers, the balloons???

UM: EARTH TO PIXEL … you didn't even notice my amazing spinny sign! I'm going to stand outside the restaurant and say J'S DINER IS OPEN FOR BUSINESS! THIS WAY!! *Spins sign hits PIXEL in the face.*

SFX: SMACK

PIXEL: Um, you hit me in the face!

UM: Sorry! Look! I also got these things for the party. *Brings out a bag of random props that have nothing to do with the party.*

PIXEL: What is all of this?

UM: Well, when I heard Grandpa say the word "PARTY" I started thinking about everything a party needs! *Pulls out items from bag and discusses how important each item is to the party. But in reality, the items have nothing to do with the party.*

PIXEL: Um, those things aren't going to help us bring in customers!

UM: Are you kidding me?! Ain't no party like an Um party! I'll have customers lined up out the door waiting to get in! We may even need to hire one of those big tough guys with sunglasses who stands in front of the door and only lets the cool people in. *Puts on sunglasses and acts like a bouncer.* Hey you, I like your shoe strings, you're in!

PIXEL: What? No, Um we don't need any of those things!

UM: Ummm ... Earth to Pixel, if we don't have all this cool stuff, what do you plan on using to throw this party?!

PIXEL: Um, didn't you listen to Grandpa J?

UM: Um ... *being very obvious that she was not listening.* Of course I listened to Grandpa J! He wanted us to throw a fantastic party to save the diner.

PIXEL: Well ... If you had really listened, you would know that Grandpa J has already provided us with everything we need to have this party.

UM: Wait, you mean Grandpa J already gave us EVERYTHING we need?

PIXEL: Yes! People are going to be here anytime now!

UM: Oh no, what are we gonna do?

Grandpa J Video 2

GRANDPA J: Well, hey hey hey! It's a great day with Grandpa J! How's the party coming along? Um, it looks like nothing has changed there ... . What's going on Um and Pixel?!

PIXEL: Well ... People are definitely going to be coming! So that's a plus! All sorts of people have been talking about it online and are super excited to see the Diner!

GRANDPA J: That's great Pixel! Um, have you set up anything yet? I have provided everything you need for the party. Did you not find it? It's in the back warehouse ...

UM: Well, I ... I ... Ummm ... Might have not listened and that caused me to not realize you had provided everything. I tried to do it on my own and didn't realize you provided the supplies I would need, and if I just listened to you and followed your direction, then this would have all been taken care of. Sorry Grandpa!

GRANDPA J: I appreciate your excitement. But from now on, I really need you to focus on what I tell you. I'm here to help you and provide for you two. Look to me and I can help you get this party done! Just in the same way that I have provided the materials that you will need for the party, the Lord always provides everything we need in life! Always remember that, The Lord is our Provider! Can you all say that?

UM & PIXEL: The Lord is Our Provider!

GRANDPA J: Great job, kiddos. Now, you best get busy!

UM: Thanks, grandpa! Bye!!

Grandpa J Video 2 ends

UM: I'm sorry Pixel, I should've listened to Grandpa J and realized he would provide everything we need.

PIXEL: That's okay Um. Now c'mon, let's go find those supplies and get busy for this party!! I can't wait to meet all these new customers and get the word out about the UPSIS!!

UM: Alright! We're gonna save the diner!!

SFX: EXIT MUSIC

Both exit.

GAME VIDEO

SONG   *Lead the congregation in a fun worship song.*

BIBLE LESSON

BIBLE LESSON INTRO VIDEO

 INTRO

Read Psalm 23:1-2 together.

Last time, we learned that David wrote Psalm 23 as a song of praise to God. He was excited the Lord was His Boss! **Psalm 23 starts with "The Lord is my shepherd."** Jesus loves each one of us very much and wants us to choose to follow Him. He wants all of us to choose to make Him our Boss, so He can be our Good Shepherd. That is amazing! Today we are going to look at the second verse in Psalm 23.

 ## READ THE BIBLE

Psalm 23:2 says, "He makes me lie down in green pastures. He leads me beside quiet waters."

In this verse, we learn that the Lord is my Provider. You see, sheep actually have a very hard time lying down. Sheep get worried and stressed about a lot of things. They worry they will not have enough grass to eat. They worry they will not have enough water to drink. They worry that a big bad wolf will try to eat them if they lie down to rest. They worry that other lambs will pick on them. In fact, sheep worry so much about these things that they just can't get any rest until all of these problems have been solved.

That's where the shepherd comes in. The shepherd knows that his sheep need rest to be healthy. He provides plenty of good green grass for his sheep to eat. He makes sure the sheep's water supply is easy for the sheep to reach and drink. This is not always easy to do. Some of the rivers may flow too fast and be dangerous for the sheep to use as a source of water. A sheep that wades too far into dangerous waters might be swept away! Many times, shepherds build big damns in the river to make sure the water is quiet and easy for the sheep to drink.

As we will learn later, shepherds also do a lot to make sure their flock is protected from wild animals like big, bad wolves. When the shepherd is close by, sheep do not need to worry about anything attacking them. They know their shepherd will provide protection. Shepherds also help when lambs start to be mean to each other. The lambs all want to be the most important, so they will hit each other in the head to show everyone how strong they are. A good shepherd will watch over his flock to keep them from hitting each other. In fact, sheep will not hit each other as long as the shepherd is present.

The more I learn about sheep, the more I think we are a lot like them. We worry about things, too, don't we? We worry about what other people think about us. We worry about who will be friends with us or play with us on the playground. We worry about the grades we are making in school. We worry about things that happen at home with our parents or brothers and sisters. Sometimes, we even worry about what is packed in our lunchboxes – I sure hope it's not leftovers from last night!!!

Jesus is our Good Shepherd. And like a shepherd, we do not need to worry about anything when He is around!

In Matthew 6:25-27 Jesus says, "I tell you, do not worry. Don't worry about your life and what you will eat or drink. And don't worry about your body and what you will wear. Isn't there more to life than eating? Aren't there more important things for the body than clothes? Look at the birds of the air. They don't plant or gather crops. They don't put away crops in storerooms. But your Father who is in heaven feeds them. Aren't you worth much more than they are? Can you add even one hour to your life by worrying?"

I love that last verse – worrying doesn't help anything! Worrying about what is in my lunchbox will not change what is in my lunchbox. Worrying about my friends will not help me make good friends! In fact, people sometimes get so busy worrying that they have a hard time doing anything else. We worry so much about taking the big test that we have a hard time studying. We worry so much about what others think that we have a hard time treating people the way God wants us to treat others.

But it is hard to stop worrying. How can we stop?

Jesus tells us in Matthew 6:33-34. "But put God's kingdom first. Do what he wants you to do. Then all of those things will also be given to you. So don't worry about tomorrow. Tomorrow will worry about itself. Each day has enough trouble of its own."

Jesus tells us to focus on God and take things one day at a time. We can replace our worry with worship! Any time we focus on God, we worship Him. Focusing on God will help us not to worry, just like a sheep looking at its shepherd will help it to lie down and rest. God wants our hearts to be at rest, because He loves us.

OBJECT LESSON

(Hold up a baseball bat.)

For example, when I focus on this bat, I can balance it on one finger.

(Balance the bat on one finger, while looking at the bat and nowhere else.)

But when I look away from the bat, the bat starts to fall.

(Look away from the bat and let the bat topple. Do this a few times to illustrate your point.)

No matter how many times I try, I can't balance this bat on one finger unless I am focusing on the bat. The same is true in life. We will have to balance a lot of things: school, friends, family, sports, music – the list goes on and on! Unless we focus our hearts, our minds, and our actions on Jesus, we will fall.

APPLICATION

Today's road sign says "Rest Area." When we focus on Jesus, we do not have to worry. Jesus is our Good Shepherd. He will take care of everything we need. He will provide for us, so that we can rest our hearts from all worry.

The next time you start to worry, stop and focus on Jesus. Take some time to worship Him. Remind yourself that God is big and strong. Remind yourself that Jesus is your Provider and ask Him to help you stop worrying. Ask Him to give you rest on the inside, so you can serve Him better on the outside.

PRAY

We are now going into our time of offering. "Offering" is a big word for present. This is the time when we give our presents to the Lord, our Shepherd. We give back to God from everything He has given to us. Let's stand together and sing this song as an offering, a big present to God.

OFFERING SONG

Lead the congregation in a slower worship song.

PRAY

Lead the congregation in prayer.

MEMORY VERSE VIDEO

MEMORY VERSE

Are you ready to memorize Psalm 23? I know I am! First let's review the first verse of Psalm 23. Remember, we sing the word "Psalm", because Psalms is a book of songs. *(Review the verse using the motions you used in the previous lesson.)*

Repeat after me:
Psaaaaalm 23. *(Psaaaaalm 23)*
The Lord is my shepherd. *(The Lord is my shepherd.)*
I shall not want. *(I shall not want.)*
Great! The next verse in Psalm 23 says, "He makes me lie down in green pastures; He leads me beside quiet waters." God takes care of us, so we can rest in Him. That's amazing!

(Ask kids to give suggestions for motions to this part of the verse. Once you have decided on the motions, repeat verse 2 once together. Then say both verses together.)

Repeat after me:

Psaaaaalm 23. *(Psaaaaalm 23.)*
The Lord is my shepherd, I shall not want. *(The Lord is my shepherd, I shall not want.)*
He makes me lie down *(He makes me lie down)*
in green pastures *(in green pastures)*
He leads me beside *(He leads me beside)*
quiet waters. *(quiet waters.)*

Great job! Now let's say both verses together, starting with "Psaaaaalm 23." Three, two, one –

Psaaaaalm 23. The Lord is my shepherd, I shall not want.
He makes me lie down in green pastures
He leads me beside quiet waters.

Great job! Can you say those verses without looking at the screens? *(Take the verse off the screen and let the kids lead you in reciting the first two verses of Psalm 23.)*

Amazing! You are all so smart. Way to go!

SONG

Lead the congregation in a fun worship song.

ANNOUNCEMENTS

Use this time to encourage kids to bring friends and participate in whatever you may have coming up next.

REVIEW GAME

It's time for the REVIEW GAME!! I need one volunteer from each grade to come up on stage. I will choose people who have been listening and paying attention the whole service and want to play in our game.

Choose contestants and introduce them to the group in game show style.

During this game, your grade can win by getting very quiet when you hear the wrong answer and very loud when you hear the right answer. Each grade is going to have a different silly move and sound that you must do when you think you hear the right answer. *(Let your contestants choose a silly motion and sound for their grade.)* I hope you are ready. I hope you have been paying attention, because the game begins ... NOW!

Give kids the opportunity to do their motions and silly sounds when they hear the correct answer. Award points to the grade who is the quietest when they hear the wrong answer and participates the most when they hear the right answer.

Question 1. What is our Main Point today?

a. The Lord Is My Protector. c. The Lord Gives Me Whatever I Want.

b. The Lord Is My Provider. d. Change Your Internet Provider.

Question 2. Where can you find today's Bible lesson?

a. Genesis 23 **c. Psalm 23**

b. Hymn 23 d. Proverbs 23

Question 3. Who wrote Psalm 23?

a. David c. Peter

b. Jonathon d. A baby goat

Option: Find a short video clip of a baby goat screaming online. Play this short clip every time you use "baby goat" as a choice. Act surprised and confused every time it plays. Let the kids laugh, then repeat the question again.

Question 4: Psalm 23:2a says, "He makes me _____ in green pastures."

a. jump **c. lie down**

b. do cartwheels d. eat like a baby goat

Question 5: Psalm 23:2b says, "He leads me beside _____."

a. quiet pastors c. stormy waters

b. quiet waters d. baby goats

Question 6: Psalm 23:1 says, "The Lord is my Shepherd. I shall not _____."

a. ... forget this verse. **c. ... want.**

b. ... panic. d. ... eat donuts.

Question 7: What is a provider?

a. Someone who gives c. A "pro" video gamer
you everything you want **d. Someone who gives you everything**
b. Someone who ignores you **you need**

SONG

Lead the congregation in a fun worship song.

DISMISSAL

LESSON 3

MAIN POINT The Lord Is My Guide.

SCRIPTURE Psalm 23:3; Psalm 25:4-5; John 10:1-5

MEMORY VERSE Psalm 23

"The Lord is my shepherd, I shall not want.
He makes me lie down in green pastures;
He leads me beside quiet waters.
He restores my soul; He guides me in the paths of
righteousness for His name's sake.
Even though I walk through the valley of the shadow of death,
I fear no evil, for You are with me;
Your rod and Your staff, they comfort me.
You prepare a table before me in the presence of my enemies;
You have anointed my head with oil; My cup overflows.
Surely goodness and lovingkindness will follow me all the
days of my life, and I will dwell in the house of the Lord forever."

TODAY'S SPECIAL

PSALM 23:3

43

THE PANTRY

LESSON 3

OVERVIEW

SPIRITUAL CONNECTION:

One of the customers in J's Diner was very lost. Pixel and Um helped the customer find their way. In Psalm 23, we learn the Lord is our Guide. Whether it is something big or something small, He always knows what direction we should take in every area of our lives.

CHARACTERS:

PIXEL - Tech savvy, music loving, older brother of Um

UM - Talkative, story-telling, fun-loving, younger sister of Pixel

CUSTOMER 1 - New customer to J's Diner

CUSTOMER 2 - Lost and ridiculously frazzled, only wants to find the way to the zoo

COSTUMES:

PIXEL - Orange shirt, jeans, white apron, and diner hat

UM - Purple shirt, jeans, white apron, and diner hat

CUSTOMER 1 - Everyday attire

CUSTOMER 2 - Disheveled everyday attire

PROPS:

- Sandwich for customer to eat (Skit)
- Prize (Bible Lesson)
- Blindfold (Bible Lesson)

LEADER DEVOTION • • • • •

PSALM 23:1-3 & PSALM 25:4-5.

Sheep are creatures of habit and are therefore known to be among the most destructive livestock on earth. Left to themselves, sheep will walk the same paths, grazing the same fields, until the grass is damaged at the root. Overgrazed fields lose their fertility and become breeding grounds for pests. It is the job of the shepherd to regularly guide his sheep to new fields, protecting the fields from overgrazing and the flock from starvation.

Aren't you glad to have a Shepherd who diligently works to break you of your destructive habits in order to lead you to greener pastures? Though we often find it very difficult to break away from our sinful, destructive habits, we can trust that Jesus, our Good Shepherd, is guiding us to a better way of life. God wants us to walk in righteousness, because living His way benefits both Him and His people. When we live in righteousness, we are free and bring glory to His Name.

The laws in the Bible are often portrayed as a laundry list of do's and don't's pushed on people by an indifferent God. But this picture of God is short-sighted and could not be further from the truth! God's desire for our righteousness is a picture of His love for us. **Proverbs 14:12 says, "There is a path before each person that seems right, but it ends in death."** In contrast, Jesus says in **John 10:10, "The thief's purpose is to steal and kill and destroy. My purpose is to give them a rich and satisfying life."** Choosing to make Jesus your guide is choosing to live abundantly!

Who or what guides your decisions each day? How do you ensure you are constantly open to the Lord's instruction? Take time this week to pray that God will continually make you teachable as He guides you to greener pastures in your relationship with Him.

Pray the kids in your group will come to know Jesus as their Guide. Pray that they would begin to understand His love for them as they learn each day to follow the guidance of their loving Shepherd.

PRE-SERVICE

Play a combination of upbeat music and fun video elements before worship begins. Encourage your JUMP Team to welcome kids and engage them in conversation.

COUNTDOWN VIDEO

JUMP Worship is starting! Lead the congregation in counting down. Worshiping together is fun, and we are ready to begin!

SONG

Lead the congregation in a fun worship song.

MAIN POINT VIDEO

WELCOME

Welcome to JUMP! Does anyone remember why we come to JUMP? We come to JUMP to worship God together. In everything we do, we can worship God by focusing on Him and giving Him first place in our lives. I cannot wait to start another fun day at J's Diner with all of you!

Today our main point is "The Lord Is My Guide." A guide teaches you which way to go. Jesus is our Guide in life. He teaches us to live His right way. He loves us and knows what is best for us.

(Make motions to help kids understand the Main Point. Repeat the Main Point a few times together before continuing.)

We are here to worship God, and we have a few rules to help us do just that. Rule number one is STAY QUIET. This rule reminds us to listen when someone is talking. Sometimes, you can hear everything that is said while you whisper to someone else, but hearing is different from really listening. Because we are here to worship, we want everyone to listen with their heads and their hearts. You can't listen when you are talking or someone is talking to you, so stay quiet. Rule number two is KEEP YOUR HANDS AND FEET TO YOURSELF. Do not distract the people around you from worshiping God! Instead of using your hands and feet to bother people, use your hands and feet to worship God. Rule number three is STAND DURING SONGS. When you hear a song, stand and worship with us. JUMP is not a show! We want everyone to participate in worship with your heads, your hearts, and everything you have! The last rule is — say it with me - HAVE FUN! We are definitely going to have fun today at J's Diner!

Let's start JUMP right by talking to God in prayer. Everyone bow your heads and close your eyes. We bow our heads to show respect, and we close our eyes to help us focus on God alone.

PRAY

Lead the congregation in prayer.

SONG

Lead the congregation in a fun worship song.

JUMP SKIT

See skit script beginning on page 50.

LESSON 3 SKIT
THE LORD IS MY GUIDE

PIXEL: Working at J's Diner has been SO much fun!

UM: Ummm, I know. We're finally getting more customers!

PIXEL: It was cool to throw that party yesterday and to make the...

PIXEL & UM: Ummy Panini Secret Ingredient Sandwich!

UM: Or the U-P-S-I-S ... the UPSIS!

PIXEL: What's UPSIS?

UM: I don't know, what's up with you? **SFX: RIM SHOT** It's the sandwich, silly!

PIXEL: One UPSIS coming right up! It just rolls off the tongue!

UM: Um, I know! With our powers combined, we made the best sandwich EVER!!! Everyone at the party loved it!

PIXEL: Grandpa provided everything we needed to make that party a success! He has taught us so much so far this summer! Most importantly, we've learned the Lord is our Provider and our Shepherd! He loves us and provides everything we need!!

Grandpa J Video 1

GRANDPA J: Well, hey hey hey! It's a great day with Grandpa J! How are my favorite grandkids doing?

UM & PIXEL: GREAT!

GRANDPA J: Glad to hear it! That party you guys helped throw yesterday was a huge hit! I really think we are going to get the diner up and running again and get all new customers! I am so thankful for your help! Now that Ummy Panini Secret Ingredient Sandwich is all the rage! Make sure you have those hot and ready for all our customers! They're sure to be flying off the stove!

UM & PIXEL: You got it, Grandpa!

GRANDPA J: Now kiddos, the most important thing I want you to remember today is that the Lord will guide you in every area of your life! Whether it's something small or something big, the Lord always wants to guide us but that means we must follow Him! Remember, The Lord is my Guide! Can you all say that?

UM & PIXEL: The Lord is my Guide!

GRANDPA J: Great job! I'll see you two later!

Grandpa J Video 1 ends

UM: Pixel, why don't you start making our special sandwich. I'll stay out here and greet our customers.

PIXEL: Great idea, Um!

Begins to exit and sees customer walking onstage.

SFX: DOOR CHIME

PIXEL: UM! We've got our first customer of the day! You know what its time for … .

UM: J'S JIVIN' JINGLE!

SFX: J'S DINER JINGLE

At end of jingle, CUSTOMER 1 applauds.

CUSTOMER 1: Bravo, bravo! Is this the place where I can order a Ummy Panini Secret Ingredient Sandwich?

UM: Yes! Home of the Ummy Panini Secret Ingredient Sandwich … or as we like to call it …

UM & PIXEL: … the UPSIS!

CUSTOMER 1: I'd like to place an order. One UPSIS please with a side of chips!

UM: One UPSIS coming right up! *(Yells backstage)* ONE UPSIS, PLEASE!

PIXEL exits, returns with the order.

PIXEL: One UPSIS with a bag of chips! *(hands bag to UM)*

UM: Here ya go! Thanks for coming in!

CUSTOMER 1: Wowee! This is definitely "all that and a bag of chips"! SFX: RIM SHOT
Exits as eating sandwich.

PIXEL: We sure make a great team! This is going great! Nothing could go wrong!

SFX: DOOR CHIME

PIXEL: Well, well, well, looks like we've got our second customer!

SFX: J'S DINER JINGLE

After jingle, UM and PIXEL hold pose, really cheesy, as they wait for an applause and Customer 2 stares at them in complete confusion.

CUSTOMER 2: *Walks in upset and disgruntled.* WHERE IN THE WORLD AM I?!?

UM and PIXEL are staying in the happiest of moods.

UM: Hello there! Where are you? You're at Grandpa J's Diner ... home of the Ummy Panini Secret Ingredient Sandwich?

CUSTOMER 2: The what?!?!?

PIXEL: The Ummy Panini Secret Ingredient Sandwich... we also like to call it the...

UM & PIXEL: UPSIS

CUSTOMER 2: UPSIS WHAT?!?!? I didn't mean to end up here!

UM: Well we sure are glad you are here! We can make you an UPSIS hot and ready!

CUSTOMER 2: I don't want an UPSIS! Or a down-sis or any sis!

PIXEL: I've got a sis. In fact, 75% of us have one. SFX: RIM SHOT

UM: Hahaha! *Realizes joke was about her.* Wait! Pixel!!!

PIXEL: Wait - I've got more jokes.... he doesn't want an UPSIS... because (s)he's UPSET

SFX: RIM SHOT

UM: Hahaha! Well, nice customer, where were you trying to end up if you weren't trying to end up here?!?

CUSTOMER 2: I was driving to the local grocery store to pick up some zucchini when suddenly I realized I actually hate zucchini! So then, I gave up on vegetables forever. I mean, who would want that when you can have ice cream?? So I went to the ice cream store, and I was next in line for a giant cone of delicious rocky road when I remembered I am lactose intolerant – which means I can't even have ice cream! That… that wouldn't have ended well. And then I was about to give up, when I decided I wanted a Thanksgiving turkey. But then I realized it isn't even Thanksgiving. So that's when I started thinking about my favorite animal – which is kind of like a turkey – it's an ostrich. The only place you can see an ostrich is the zoo! I tried to get to the zoo on my own, but I ended up here! I just want to see an ostrich! IS THAT TOO MUCH TO ASK?!? *(Dramatically on the floor throwing a fit.)*

PIXEL: Wow.

UM: Now (s)he tells a good story!

PIXEL: Let's start at the very beginning.

UM: A very good place to start.

PIXEL: You want to see an ostrich. Am I understanding you?

CUSTOMER 2: Yes! I just want to see an ostrich.

UM: First, let me ask you, are you're hungry? Would you like an UPSIS?

CUSTOMER 2: Ya know what … sure … why not?!? What else do I have to lose at this point!? I've been trying to get to the zoo for HOURS!

UM: I'll go make the UPSIS. BRB! *Exits.*

PIXEL: Let's take a seat. Now, why did you want to see an ostrich?

CUSTOMER 2: Well, like I said, an ostrich is my favorite animal, and the only place you can see one is the zoo.

PIXEL: Why were you thinking about an ostrich?

CUSTOMER 2: Like I said, I was driving to the local grocery store to pick up some zucchini when suddenly I realized I actually hate zucchini …

PIXEL: Never mind. I forgot how long that story was. Let me help you … I know you're stressed. I get stressed, too. When I get stressed, I pray. You can always pray for God's guidance.

CUSTOMER 2: You're right! I should have prayed earlier instead of panicking.

PIXEL: I'VE GOT IT! Here look at this … I've got this thing called a GPS.

CUSTOMER 2: A GPS? Does that stand for a Great Pizza Smell?

PIXEL: Uh, no.

CUSTOMER 2: A Guinea Pig's Sister?

PIXEL: No.

CUSTOMER 2: OH I'VE GOT IT! A Gentle Pedestrian Stressed out because they can't find the zoo!!

PIXEL: A GPS. It stands for the Global Positioning System. It will help get you where you need to go! See?

`Video of GPS` *Video starts with J's Diner logo and shows a few streets to get to the zoo.*

PIXEL: Look, the zoo isn't that far at all! Why don't I take you to the zoo? I'd love to help guide you there!

CUSTOMER 2: That would be FANTASTIC!

UM enters on stage.

UM: Someone want an UPSIS?!?

PIXEL: You know sis! `SFX: RIM SHOT`

CUSTOMER 2: Thanks so much for your help!

PIXEL: Let's get you to the zoo to find that ostrich!

All exit.

`GAME VIDEO`

`SONG` *Lead the congregation in a fun worship song.*

BIBLE LESSON

 INTRO

David wrote Psalm 23 as a song of praise to God. Before he became one of the greatest kings of Israel, David was a shepherd. He knew a lot about the relationship between sheep and their shepherd. He knew that sheep depend on their shepherd the same way that we depend on God. Having the Lord as your shepherd is a very good thing!

Read Psalm 23:1-3 together.

 ## READ THE BIBLE

Psalm 23:3 says, "He restores my soul. He guides me in paths of righteousness for His name's sake."

Shepherds have to regularly move their sheep to new fields. If shepherds were to let sheep stay in the same field, the flock would eat all of the grass. In fact, they would eat so much of the grass that it would be hard for grass to grow in that field ever again! To protect his sheep, the shepherd has to guide his flock to new fields. He guides them in the right paths.

In life, Jesus is our Good Shepherd. He guides us in the right paths, too. Of course we can't literally follow Jesus around here on earth. But we can live His way, the way He laid out for us in the Bible. The word "righteous" means "right with God." Jesus guides us and leads us in life to live in right relationship with God. He wants us to live God's way, because it is best for us.

What would happen if a lamb decided not to follow his shepherd? What if he decided to stay in the field while his shepherd lead the flock to a different field? The sheep might feel very happy for a little while. He would have all the grass to himself! But without the shepherd, the lamb would be open to attack by wild animals. He would be helpless against the bugs that bother him every day. After a while, the grass would run out, and the sheep would not know where to go for food. The lamb should have stayed with his shepherd!

What happens when we do not follow Jesus in the righteous, right, way to live? When we choose to sin, it might feel really fun for a little while. For example, let's say you choose to cheat on a test. At first, you feel great because you made a good grade! But then, everyone starts congratulating you and asking you to help them study for the next test. Your parents are proud of you for doing so well and studying so hard, but you feel awful on the inside. Because you didn't study for the last test, you don't really understand what the teacher is teaching now. In order to get the same great grade on the next test, you think you might have to cheat again. You don't want to, but you don't see any way out. What are you going to do? You shouldn't have cheated on that test.

Maybe you didn't cheat, but you chose to lie, disobey your parents, or be mean to a brother or sister. Every time we choose to do something wrong, we are choosing to sin. Sin separates us from God, and that is definitely not good for us!

Thankfully, Jesus loves us so much that He made a way for us to come back to Him. Jesus died on the cross for our sins and came back to life three days later, so those who choose Him can be forgiven and have a relationship with God again. Jesus really is a Good Shepherd!!

Sheep often fall upside down on their backs and can't get up. An upside down lamb is called a cast sheep. It sounds like a silly problem at first, but it is actually very serious. If a lamb cannot get back up in a certain amount of time, the sheep will die. When a good shepherd sees a cast sheep, he will run to help the sheep turn right side up.

In the same way, even after choosing to make Jesus the Boss of our lives, we sometimes make mistakes. We choose to sin.

1 John 1:9 says, "If we confess our sins, He is faithful and just to forgive us our sins and to cleanse us from all unrighteousness."

When we tell Jesus about our sins and ask Him to forgive us, He will forgive us and help us back on our feet again. Jesus, the Good Shepherd, will guide us back to the righteous, right path, because He loves us and wants what is best for us.

 ## OBJECT LESSON

(Choose one volunteer to wear a blindfold. Once you have blindfolded the person, hand a prize to a JUMP Team Member. Have the JUMP Team Member stand

somewhere in the room where everyone can see them, but not where it would be easy for the blindfolded person to find them on their own.)

I have given someone in this room a great prize. I want you to find that person. When you find that person, you can have the prize. I need everyone in the room to be very quiet. Don't tell them where the prize is!

(Let the blindfolded person search for a few seconds, then offer to guide them to the prize. When they have received the prize, let them sit back down.)

God has great treasures for us in Heaven. He wants us to see the long-lasting prize that comes from living His way. When we let Jesus guide us in living the right way, we can have great rewards! The rules in the Bible are not just there for fun. God gave us the Bible to tell us about His Son, Jesus, and how to live God's way, because He loves us very much.

APPLICATION

Today's road sign is a U-Turn sign. When we sin, Jesus wants us to make a U-Turn. Tell Jesus that you are sorry for doing the wrong thing. Ask Him to guide you in doing the right thing from now on, and He will! Jesus is a Good Shepherd who will guide you in the righteous, right way.

Psalm 25:4-5 says, "Make me know Your ways, O Lord; teach me Your paths. Lead me in Your truth and teach me, for You are the God of my salvation; for You I wait all the day."

I pray that we will all ask Jesus to teach us every day how to love Him by the way we live. I challenge you this week to start every day by asking Jesus to teach you how to live His way.

PRAY

We are now going into our time of offering. "Offering" is a big word for present. This is the time when we give our presents to the Lord, our Shepherd. We give back to God from everything He has given to us. Let's stand together and sing this song as an offering, a big present to God.

OFFERING SONG

Lead the congregation in a slower worship song.

PRAY

Lead the congregation in prayer.

MEMORY VERSE VIDEO

MEMORY VERSE

Are you ready to memorize Psalm 23? I know I am! First let's review what we have learned already. Remember, we sing the word "Psalm", because Psalms is a book of songs. *(Review the verses using the motions you used in the previous lessons.)*

Repeat after me:
Psaaaaalm 23. *(Psaaaaalm 23)*
The Lord is my shepherd. I shall not want. *(The Lord is my shepherd. I shall not want.)*
He makes me lie down in green pastures. *(He makes me lie down in green pastures.)*
He leads me beside quiet waters. *(He leads me beside quiet waters.)*

Great! The next verse in Psalm 23 says, "He restores my soul; He guides me in paths of righteousness for His name's sake." I am so glad Jesus is a Good Shepherd, who leads us away from the wrong choices that hurt us and toward the right path in life. When we live His righteous, right way, we honor Him. Living His way is one way we worship God.

(Ask kids to give suggestions for motions to this part of the verse. Once you have decided on the motions, repeat verse 3 once together. Then say the verses together.)

Repeat after me:
Psaaaaalm 23. *(Psaaaaalm 23)*
The Lord is my shepherd. I shall not want. *(The Lord is my shepherd. I shall not want.)*
He makes me lie down in green pastures. *(He makes me lie down in green pastures.)*
He leads me beside quiet waters. *(He leads me beside quiet waters.)*

He restores my soul; *(He restores my soul;)*
He guides me *(He guides me)*

in the paths of righteousness *(in the paths of righteousness)*
For His name's sake. *(For His name's sake.)*

Great job! Now let's say it all together together, starting with "Psaaaaalm 23." Three, two, one –

Psaaaaalm 23. The Lord is my shepherd, I shall not want.
He makes me lie down in green pastures
He leads me beside quiet waters.
He restores my soul;
He guides me in paths of righteousness for His name's sake.

Great job! Can you say those verses without looking at the screens? This is a lot, so let's jump up and down to get ready. *(Jump up and down a few times.)* Are you ready? Let's do this! *(Take the verse off the screen and let the kids lead you in reciting the first two verses of Psalm 23.)*

Amazing! You are all so smart. Way to go!

SONG

Lead the congregation in a fun worship song.

ANNOUNCEMENTS

Use this time to encourage kids to bring friends and participate in whatever you may have coming up next.

REVIEW GAME

It's time for the REVIEW GAME!! I need one volunteer from each grade to come up on stage. I will choose people who have been listening and paying attention the whole service and want to play in our game.

Choose contestants and introduce them to the group in game show style.

During this game, your grade can win by getting very quiet when you hear the wrong answer and very loud when you hear the right answer. Each grade is going to have a different silly move and sound that you must do when you think you hear the right answer. *(Let your contestants choose a silly motion and sound for their grade.)*

I hope you are ready. I hope you have been paying attention, because the game begins ... NOW!

Give kids the opportunity to do their motions and silly sounds when they hear the correct answer. Award points to the grade who is the quietest when they hear the wrong answer and participates the most when they hear the right answer.

Question 1. What is our Main Point today?
- a. The Lord Is My GPS.
- **b. The Lord Is My Guide.**
- c. Lloyd Is My Pet Gorilla.
- d. Use a Map, so You Won't Get Lost.

Question 2. Where can you find today's Bible lesson?
- a. Proverbs 23
- b. Pancake 23
- **c. Psalm 23**
- d. Penelope 23

Question 3. Who wrote Psalm 23?
- **a. David**
- b. Jonathon
- c. Peter
- d. A baby goat

Option: Find a short video clip of a baby goat screaming online. Play this short clip every time you use "baby goat" as a choice. Act surprised and confused every time it plays. Let the kids laugh, then repeat the question again.

Question 4: Psalm 23:3 says, "He restores my soul; He guides me in the _____ for His name's sake."
- **a. paths of righteousness**
- b. paths of ripe bananas
- c. paths with lots of people
- d. paths of baby goats

Question 5: Psalm 23:2 says, "He makes me lie down in green pastures. He leads me beside _____."
- a. quiet pastors
- **b. quiet waters**
- c. stormy waters
- d. baby goats

Question 6: Psalm 23:1 says, "The Lord is my Shepherd. I shall not _____."
- a. ... forget this verse.
- b. ... panic.
- **c. ... want.**
- d. ... eat donuts.

Question 7: What is righteousness?

    a. Making right turns only

    b. Something radically awesome

    c. Being right-handed

    d. Living God's right way

SONG

Lead the congregation in a fun worship song.

DISMISSAL

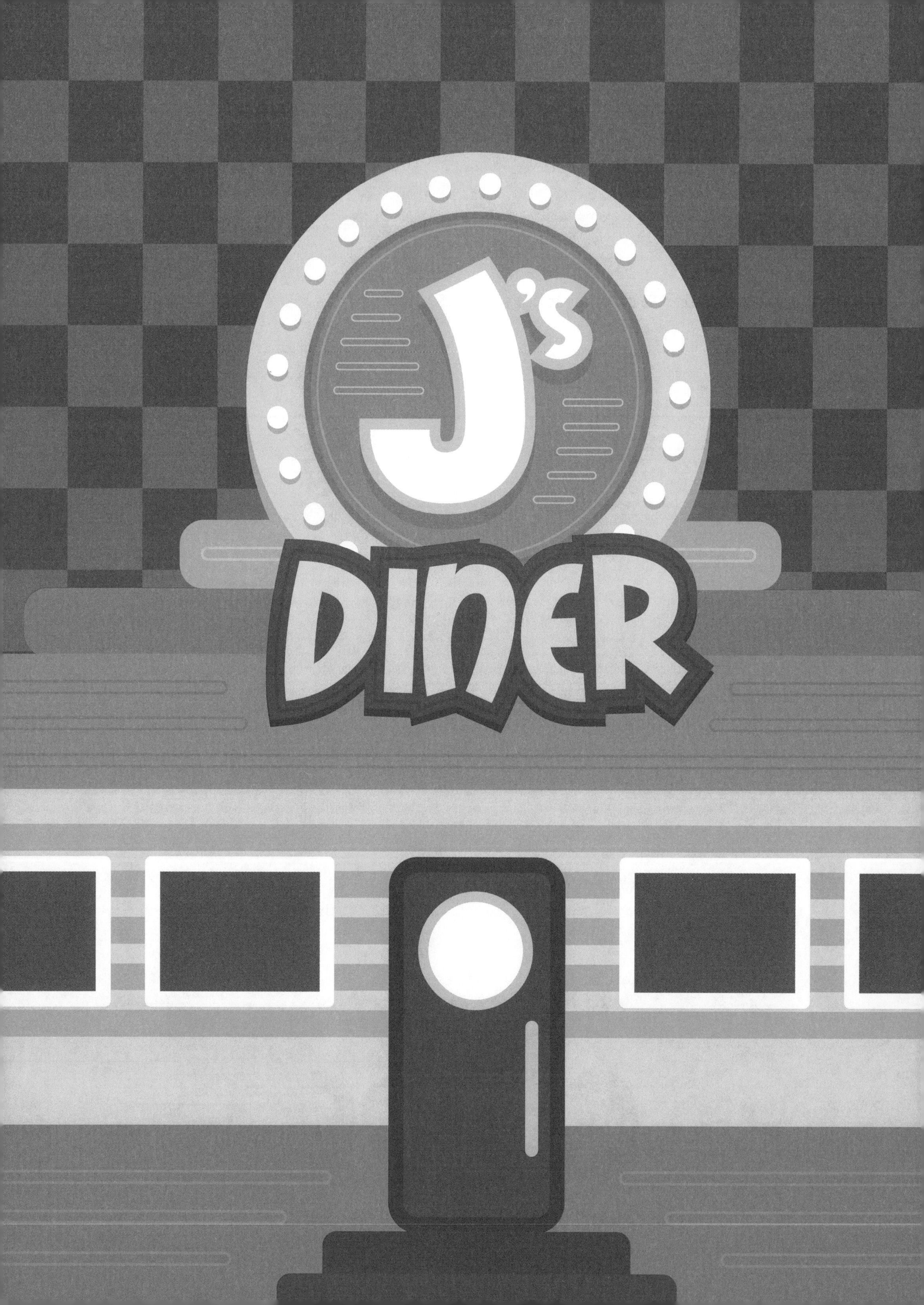
J's
DINER

LESSON 4

MAIN POINT The Lord Is My Protector.

SCRIPTURE Psalm 23:4a; John 10:11-18

MEMORY VERSE Psalm 23

"The Lord is my shepherd, I shall not want.
He makes me lie down in green pastures;
He leads me beside quiet waters.
He restores my soul; He guides me in the paths of
righteousness for His name's sake.
**Even though I walk through the valley of the shadow of death,
I fear no evil, for You are with me;**
Your rod and Your staff, they comfort me.
You prepare a table before me in the presence of my enemies;
You have anointed my head with oil; My cup overflows.
Surely goodness and lovingkindness will follow me all the
days of my life, and I will dwell in the house of the Lord forever."

TODAY'S SPECIAL

PSALM 23:4A

THE PANTRY

LESSON 4

OVERVIEW

SPIRITUAL CONNECTION:

When a big thunderstorm hits J's Diner and the power goes out, Pixel and Um are scared. Thankfully, Grandpa J sends a police officer to check on them. The police officer protects them during the storm. In Psalm 23, we learn the Lord is our Protector. Sometimes we will have days that are sunny outside, but stormy in life. Even on our worst days, we remember God is our Protector, and He is always with us.

CHARACTERS:

PIXEL - Tech savy, music loving, older brother of Um

UM - Talkative, story-telling, fun-loving, younger sister of Pixel

POLICEMAN PETE - Confident and kind, helps Pixel and Um calm down

COSTUMES:

PIXEL - Orange shirt, jeans, white apron, and diner hat

UM - Purple shirt, jeans, white apron, and diner hat

POLICEMAN PETE - Police jacket and hat, Blue dress pants

PROPS:

- Police costume for pastor (Skit)
- Bible (Skit)

LEADER DEVOTION • • • • •

PSALM 23:4A & JOHN 10:11-18.

Up to this point in Psalm 23, David has been boasting about the strengths of His shepherd to others. **In verse 4,** the psalm shifts to a more personal tone. Instead of talking about his Shepherd, David starts to speak to his Shepherd. At the same time, the scene shifts from peaceful waters and green pastures to **"the valley of the shadow of death."**

Every summer in hill country, shepherds drive their flocks to new pastures at a higher elevation. Every autumn, these same shepherds drive their flocks back down to the lower pastures. Shepherds often walk these journeys ahead of the sheep to ensure they are prepared for all potential hazards. The journey can be very hazardous, as shepherds may need to fight wild animals and fend off potential thieves. The only thing familiar to the habit-loving sheep is their shepherd. They rely on Him for protection.

Psalm 23:4 does not say, "If I walk through the valley," but **"Even though I walk through the valley ... ."** God does not promise His children the absence of hard times; He promises His presence through the valleys of our lives. On your darkest day, Jesus is there with you in the valley. His presence and power are promises - facts. If you are going through a valley right now in your life, be encouraged knowing God is always with you, whether or not you can "feel" His presence. And like the good shepherds, He has walked these roads ahead of you. Know your valley has not caught the Lord by surprise. He is prepared to protect you and guide you to higher places in your relationship with Him. You do not need to fear.

Take time to thank Jesus for being the Good Shepherd who **"lays down His life for the sheep." (John 10:11)** Thank Him for His sacrifice for you. Praise Him for His power and His presence in every situation. Ask Him to teach you to trust Him.

Pray over the kids in your group. You may never know what "valleys" they are going through or will go through in their lifetimes, but you can be sure the Lord will be with His children. Pray they will come to know Jesus as their Lord and Savior. Pray they will learn to trust Him in every situation, so that they do not need to be afraid.

LESSON 4

PRE-SERVICE

Play a combination of upbeat music and fun video elements before worship begins. Encourage your JUMP Team to welcome kids and engage them in conversation.

COUNTDOWN VIDEO

JUMP Worship is starting! Lead the congregation in counting down. Worshiping together is fun, and we are ready to begin!

SONG

Lead the congregation in a fun worship song.

MAIN POINT VIDEO

WELCOME

Welcome to JUMP! I cannot wait to start another fun day at J's Diner with all of you! Today our main point is "The Lord Is My Protector." Our God is strong! He can protect us from any danger.

(Make motions to help kids understand the Main Point. Repeat the Main Point a few times together before continuing.)

Great job! Before we get started, does anyone remember why we come to JUMP? That's right! We come to JUMP to worship God together. We have a few rules to help us focus on God alone and put Him first. Does anyone know rule number one? Rule number one is STAY QUIET. Show me what it should sound like in this room when someone like me is talking. *(Wait for the group to become very quiet.)* You all know exactly what to do. Great job! God has something to say to you and me, and we do not want to miss it, because we are talking. Rule number two is KEEP YOUR HANDS AND FEET TO YOURSELF. Instead of using your hands and feet to bother people, use your hands and feet to worship God. Following this rule will help us focus on God and not on the people around us. Rule number three is STAND DURING SONGS. When you hear a song, stand and worship with us. JUMP is not a show! We want everyone to participate in worship with us! The last rule is – say it with me – HAVE FUN! We are definitely going to have fun today at J's Diner!

Let's get started by talking to our great and amazing God in prayer. Everyone bow your heads and close your eyes. We bow our heads to show respect, and we close our eyes to help us focus on God alone.

PRAY

Lead the congregation in prayer.

SONG

Lead the congregation in a fun worship song.

JUMP SKIT

See skit script beginning on page 68.

THE LORD IS MY PROTECTOR

LESSON 4 SKIT
THE LORD IS MY PROTECTOR

PIXEL and UM are cleaning the diner.

PIXEL: Wow. It's been so busy here at J's Diner lately. I hope we're making Grandpa happy!

UM: I know we've been working so hard to get the word out about how great J's Diner is!

PIXEL: We gotta get this place cleaned up, so it looks fresh and clean for all our customers tomorrow!

PIXEL starts to clean. UM is still talking.

UM: I know! This summer has been AWESOME! We've been all like "I'm making the Ummy Panini Secret Ingredient Sandwich" … and then we were all like "let's call it the UPSIS" and then you were like "one UPSIS coming right up" and then we had tons of customers and then we sang J's Jivin' Diner Song …

SFX: J'S DINER JINGLE *UM sings and dances by herself energetically.*

UM: And then we had tons more customers and everything was going well and then…

SFX: THUNDERCLAP *Both fall to the floor.*

UM: Ahhhhhh!

PIXEL: Calm down! You're okay! It's just rain. Nothing to worry about.

SFX: THUNDERCLAP

UM: Ahhhhhhh HELP ME!!!

PIXEL: Um. You gotta take a chill pill.

SFX: THUNDERCLAP

UM: I'm NOT calm. I'm NOT calm!!!!

PIXEL: Calm down, calm down. It's only thunder. I did read online that a storm was coming. But we don't need to panic unless there's lightning.

SFX: THUNDERCLAP *Lights flicker to resemble lightning.*

UM & PIXEL: Panic! Lightning! *Run around in panic and end in a scared, funny position.*

Grandpa J Video 1

> **GRANDPA J:** Well, hey hey hey! It's a great day with Grandpa J! Looks like you guys are getting the place spic and span! *(Video starts to go in and out like it's losing service due to storm. Thunder in the background.)* I saw a storm was coming y'all's way. Make sure you get the burners turned off and the register locked and closed down before the storm. If you only hear one thing from me today, then the most important thing you need to know is … . *(video cuts out)*

Grandpa J Video 1 ends

UM: Um um um um, Grandpa J?

PIXEL: Grandpa J? Where'd you go?! What is the most important thing?!

UM: Ahhhhhhh the storm sounds like it's getting really close! I don't like storms. This one time it was storming and mom said "make sure you have a candle, a flashlight and a can of tuna ready to go." So then I looked around and found the candle, the flashlight, but I couldn't find the tuna! So then I was like … hmm … . Where would the tuna be?! So I checked the fridge. NOPE! Not there. So I checked the pantry. NOPE! Where would mom keep the tuna? So then I finally figured it out … I found it in the …

SFX: THUNDERCLAP

PIXEL: We need to stay calm! Let me get online to see how bad this storm is going to be. *Pulls out phone.* Oh no! I don't have any service. The storm must be so bad that it's ruined the cell towers.

UM: I don't know what that means, but it sounds really, really bad!

SFX: THUNDERCLAP

UM: PIXEL!!! I'm so scared!! *Jumps in PIXEL's arms.*

PIXEL: Get off me! Listen, we need to just remain calm and do what grandpa said before he cut out. You get the register taken care of, and I'll turn off the burners.

PIXEL exits.

UM: Okay. Close the register ... I can do that ...

SFX: THUNDERCLAP *Lights turn off.*

UM: Ummm Pixel!! I can't see!!! Pixel!! Where are you??!?! I don't like the dark!! *Crawling around on the floor.*

SFX: DOOR CHIME

POLICEMAN enters.

UM: Pixel? Is that you? I heard the door ... Did you leave me here alone?! Don't leave me Pixel! Don't leave me!!!! I can't survive on my own!

PIXEL: *Yells from offstage.* I didn't leave you! I'm turning the burners off back here!

POLICEMAN: Hello? Anyone here?

UM: *Whispering to backstage* Pixel? Pixel where are you? Stranger danger! Someone is here, and I don't know who it is!

POLICEMAN: Hello? Kids? Anyone here?

UM: *Whispering louder* PIXEL! I really, really think you need to come out here!

PIXEL: What is it Um?

UM: There's someone here! Come help me!

PIXEL runs on.

POLICEMAN starts to walk around with a flashlight. PIXEL and UM follow right behind him. They eventually bump into each other and scare each other.

POLICEMAN shines flashlight on PIXEL and UM. PIXEL and UM put their hands up to surrender.

UM: We didn't do anything wrong!! We are innocent! I want my mommy!! *Jumps in PIXEL'S arms.*

POLICEMAN: Calm down, kids! My name is Policeman Pete. I'm here to help.

UM: You're a policeman? Oh. I thought you were a big scary monster that was coming to take all our UPSIS!!

SFX: DUN DUN DUN

POLICEMAN: An UPSIS?

PIXEL: The Ummy Panini Secret Ingredient Sandwich.

POLICEMAN: Oh, I've heard of that! Everyone says it's delicious! But I didn't come here for food. The storm was starting to get pretty bad, so I came to check in on you kids. I wanted to make sure you guys weren't scared.

PIXEL: I'm not THAT scared …

SFX: THUNDERCLAP

PIXEL: I take it back! We are very scared of this storm.

POLICEMAN: Don't worry! I'm here to help protect you. We are safe inside. You know what, this makes me think of who our Ultimate Protector is.

UM: Who??

POLICEMAN: The Bible says in Psalm 23:4, *Opens to Psalms 23:4a* "Even though I walk through the valley of the shadow of death, I will fear no evil, for You are with me … ." This verse reminds us that Jesus, our Shepherd, is always with us. When we walk in the darkest days or storms, Jesus is there. He is prepared to protect you and guide you. You do not need to fear. The Lord is our Protector. Lets all say that together!

PIXEL & UM: The Lord is our Protector

PIXEL: So you're saying that even though it's dark and really scary out, I can still be at peace, because God is with me?

POLICEMAN: Yes. And sometimes we will have days that are sunny outside, but stormy in life. Things may not be going well, or we might be scared of a challenge or event that is coming our way, but we must remember God is our Protector and He is always with us.

UM: Ummm wow. I feel so much better, Mr. Police Officer Man.

POLICEMAN: Just call me Pete.

PIXEL: Hey! It sounds like the storm is passing.

SFX: LIGHTS FLICKER BACK ON

POLICEMAN: It sure does! Glad to hear that sunny skies are coming back!

Grandpa J Video 2

> **GRANDPA J:** Well hey there kiddos! Looks like we got our service back! I called the police station to have them send someone to check on you kiddos. Did they make it there all right?

UM & PIXEL: Yes! He's here right now!

> **GRANDPA J:** That's great! I'm glad you all are safe and sound! Keep working hard, and I'll talk to you kiddos soon!

UM: Thanks so much Grandpa. Bye!!

Grandpa J Video 2 ends

PIXEL: But what was the most important thing you were going to tell us??

UM: *Suddenly serious and looking off into the distance.* We may never know.

PIXEL: Pete, thanks so much for your help and for making sure we were protected! You made Um feel so much better … and me too.

POLICEMAN: Glad I could help! Now … how bout you two whip me up one of those UPSIDEDOWN Cakes?

PIXEL & UM: You mean an UPSIS?

POLICEMAN: Right … one of those!

PIXEL: One UPSIS, coming right up!!

All exit.

GAME VIDEO

SONG *Lead the congregation in a fun worship song.*

BIBLE LESSON

BIBLE LESSON INTRO VIDEO

 INTRO

What do you do when you are hurt or afraid? You run to your parents! You cry for your mom! MOOMMMMMYYYYYY!!!! It's funny, but we have all done something like that. When a thunderstorm comes, a lot of kids run straight to their parents' room until the storm passes through. When they get hurt at the playground, they run to their parents or their teacher for help. When we get scared, we want to go to someone who loves us and can help us. Today's verse is all about what we do when we are afraid or hurt. Jesus is our Good Shepherd. He will take care of His children, those who have decided to put Him in charge of their lives.

 READ THE BIBLE

In Psalm 23, David explains how the Good Shepherd takes care of His sheep even in times of danger.

Read Psalm 23:1-4a together.

Psalm 23:4a says, "Even though I walk through the valley of the shadow of death, I will fear no evil, for You are with me."

In other words, when bad things happen, I will not be afraid, because I know that Jesus is with me. It is natural to panic when something bad happens. Sometimes we even start to panic just thinking about all the bad things that could happen one day. We worry about all kinds of things:

What if no one likes me at school?
What if someone makes fun of me?
What if my parents get a divorce?
What if I get sick?

What if my parents forget to pick me up after the sleepover?
What if I drop the ball in the big game?

What if?

Boys and girls, there is good news! Because of Jesus, we know the answer to every one of those questions. If no one likes you at school, Jesus is with you. He loves you very much. If someone makes fun of you, Jesus is with you. He made you and loves you just as you are. If your parents get a divorce, Jesus is still with you. He will never leave you. If your parents forget to pick you up, Jesus is still with you. He never forgets about you. If you get sick, Jesus is with you. He is the best doctor in the world, because He made you. If you drop the ball in the big game, Jesus is still with you and wants to be your friend.

No matter what happens to you in this life, Jesus will be with you! You can always run to Him when you are hurt or scared. If you have accepted Jesus' gift of forgiveness and friendship by choosing to put Him in charge of your life, Jesus will always be by your side. You never have to be afraid, because Jesus is strong enough to protect you in every kind of situation. Of course, bad things will still happen. But in every situation, Jesus will be with you.

In life, we will go through hard times. Jesus does not promise that hard things won't happen to us. Bad things will happen. Jesus does promise us something amazing, though! If you know Jesus as your Lord and Savior, He will never leave you alone. He will always be with you. A caution sign reminds us to be ready for the dangers ahead. We can be ready for hard times in life by making sure that we know Jesus! If you do not know Jesus, please talk to us before you leave today. We would love to tell you more about Him!

APPLICATION

The Lord Is Our Protector. That does not mean bad things won't happen. The "valley of the shadow of death" in Psalm 23 was actually pretty scary for the sheep. The valley could be very dark at times because of the shadows of the mountains. But the shepherd had to lead his sheep through the valleys in order to bring them to the tablelands, high places with lots of good grass to eat. Sheep had to stay close to the shepherd in the valleys, so they could eventually reach higher ground.

When bad things happen, we can trust that Jesus knows what is best for us. He is not surprised by anything that might happen, and He will never leave us. The Lord Is Our Protector!

PRAY

We are now going into our time of offering. "Offering" is a big word for present. This is the time when we give our presents to the Lord, our Shepherd. We give back to God from everything He has given to us. Let's stand together and sing this song as an offering, a big present to God.

THE LORD IS MY
PROTECTOR

OFFERING SONG

Lead the congregation in a slower worship song.

PRAY

Lead the congregation in prayer.

MEMORY VERSE VIDEO

MEMORY VERSE

Are you ready to memorize Psalm 23? I know I am! First let's review what we have learned already. Remember, we sing the word "Psalm", because Psalms is a book of songs. (*Review the verses using the motions you used in the previous lessons.*)

Repeat after me:
Psaaaaalm 23. (*Psaaaaalm 23*)
The Lord is my shepherd. I shall not want. (*The Lord is my shepherd. I shall not want.*)
He makes me lie down in green pastures. (*He makes me lie down in green pastures.*)
He leads me beside quiet waters. (*He leads me beside quiet waters.*)
He guides me in the paths of righteousness (*He guides me in the paths of righteousness*)
For His name's sake. (*For His name's sake.*)

Great! The next part of Psalm 23 says, "Even though I walk through the valley of the shadow of death, I fear no evil, for You are with me." The valley of the shadow of death does not sound like a very fun place to go. Everyone who knows Jesus as the Lord of their lives, does not need to be afraid even in a scary place like the "valley of the shadow of death," because Jesus is with them! When Jesus is with you, you do not need to be afraid.

(*Ask kids to give suggestions for motions to this part of the verse. Once you have decided on the motions, repeat verse 4a once together. Then say the verses together.*)

Repeat after me:
Psaaaaalm 23. (*Psaaaaalm 23*)
The Lord is my shepherd. I shall not want. (*The Lord is my shepherd. I shall not want.*)

He makes me lie down in green pastures. *(He makes me lie down in green pastures.)*
He leads me beside quiet waters. *(He leads me beside quiet waters.)*
He restores my soul; *(He restores my soul;)*
He guides me in the paths of righteousness *(He guides me in the paths of righteousness)*
For His name's sake. *(For His name's sake.)*

Even though I walk *(Even though I walk)*
through the valley of the shadow of death, *(through the valley of the shadow of death,)*
I fear no evil, *(I fear no evil,)*
for You are with me; *(for You are with me;)*

Great job! Now let's say it all together, starting with "Psaaaaalm 23." Three, two, one –

Psaaaaalm 23. The Lord is my shepherd, I shall not want.
He makes me lie down in green pastures
He leads me beside quiet waters.
He restores my soul;
He guides me in paths of righteousness for His name's sake.
Even though I walk through the valley of the shadow of death,
I fear no evil, for You are with me;

Great job! Can you say those verses without looking at the screens? This is a lot, so let's do a few stretches to get ready. *(Lead the group in a few stretches.)* Are you ready? Let's do this! *(Take the verses off the screen and let the kids lead you in reciting the first two verses of Psalm 23.)*

Amazing! You are all so smart. Way to go!

SONG

Lead the congregation in a fun worship song.

ANNOUNCEMENTS

Use this time to encourage kids to bring friends and participate in whatever you may have coming up next.

REVIEW GAME

It's time for the REVIEW GAME!! I need one volunteer from each grade to come up on stage. I will choose people who have been listening and paying attention the whole service and want to play in our game.

Choose contestants and introduce them to the group in game show style.

During this game, your grade can win by getting very quiet when you hear the wrong answer and very loud when you hear the right answer. Each grade is going to have a different silly move and sound that you must do when you think you hear the right answer. *(Let your contestants choose a silly motion and sound for their grade.)*

I hope you are ready. I hope you have been paying attention, because the game begins ... NOW!

Give kids the opportunity to do their motions and silly sounds when they hear the correct answer. Award points to the grade who is the quietest when they hear the wrong answer and participates the most when they hear the right answer.

Question 1. What is our Main Point today?
    a. The Lord Is My Projector.   c. The Lord Is Only With Me on Good Days.
    b. The Lord Is My Protector.   d. Stay Away from Dark Valleys.

Question 2. Where can you find today's Bible lesson?
    a. Panama 23   **c. Psalm 23**
    b. Projector 23   d. Habakkuk 23

Question 3. Who wrote Psalm 23?
    a. David   c. Peter
    b. Jonathon   d. A baby goat

Option: Find a short video clip of a baby goat screaming online. Play this short clip every time you use "baby goat" as a choice. Act surprised and confused every time it plays. Let the kids laugh, then repeat the question again.

Question 4: Psalm 23:4a says, "Even though I walk through the valley of _____, I fear no evil, for You are with me."
    a. shenanigans   c. the shadow of wolves
    b. the shadow of baby goats   **d. the shadow of death**

**Question 5: Psalm 23:3 says, "He restores my soul; He guides me in the
_____ for His name's sake."**

a. paths of righteousness   c. paths with lots of people
b. paths of ripe bananas   d. paths of baby goats

**Question 6: Psalm 23:2 says, "He makes me lie down in green pastures.
He leads me beside _____."**

a. quiet pastors   c. stormy waters
b. quiet waters   d. baby goats

Question 7: Psalm 23:1 says, "The Lord is my Shepherd. I shall not _____."

a. ... forget this verse.   **c. ... want.**
b. ... panic.   d. ... eat donuts.

SONG

Lead the congregation in a fun worship song.

DISMISSAL

THE LORD IS MY
PROTECTOR

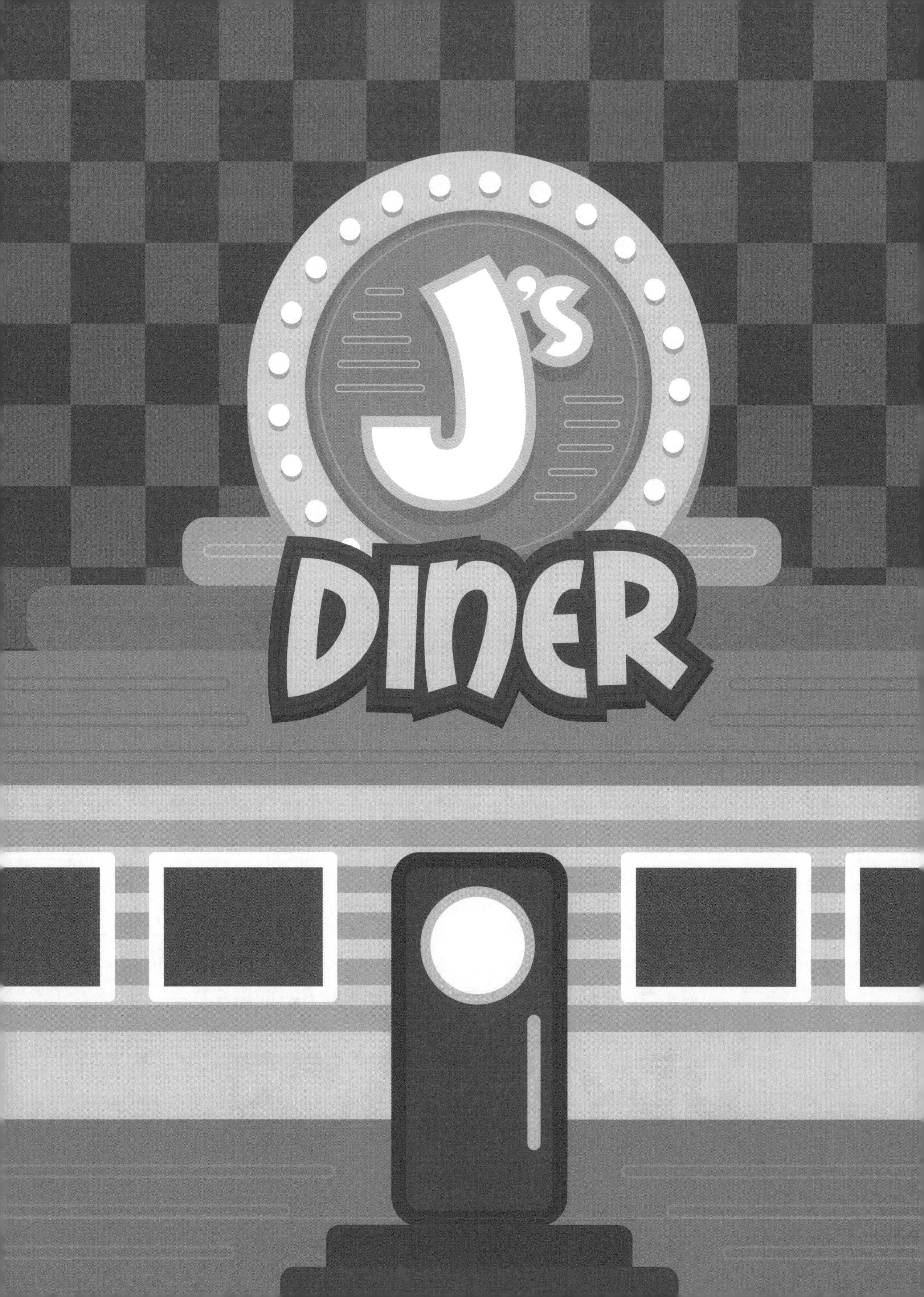
J's
DINER

LESSON 5

MAIN POINT The Lord Is in Charge.

SCRIPTURE Psalm 23:4b; Proverbs 3:1-12

MEMORY VERSE Psalm 23

"The Lord is my shepherd, I shall not want.
He makes me lie down in green pastures;
He leads me beside quiet waters.
He restores my soul; He guides me in the paths of
righteousness for His name's sake.
Even though I walk through the valley of the shadow of death,
I fear no evil, for You are with me;
Your rod and Your staff, they comfort me.
You prepare a table before me in the presence of my enemies;
You have anointed my head with oil; My cup overflows.
Surely goodness and lovingkindness will follow me all the
days of my life, and I will dwell in the house of the Lord forever."

TODAY'S SPECIAL

PSALM 23:4B

THE PANTRY

LESSON 5

OVERVIEW

SPIRITUAL CONNECTION:

Pixel tries to impress a cool kid at his school. In the process, Pixel is mean to his sister, lies about his football skills, and gives away a free meal without permission. Pixel learns Grandpa J is in charge and accepts the punishment for his wrong choices. In Psalm 23, we learn the Lord is in charge. Because He loves us, He corrects us when we are wrong. He teaches how to live His right way.

CHARACTERS:

PIXEL - Tech savy, music loving, older brother of Um

UM - Talkative, story-telling, fun-loving, younger sister of Pixel

FRIEND - Cool football player

COSTUMES:

PIXEL - Orange shirt, jeans, white apron, and diner hat

UM - Purple shirt, jeans, white apron, and diner hat

FRIEND - Letter jacket, jeans

PROPS:

- Brown bag (Skit)
- Fake $ (Skit)
- Phone (Skit)
- Menu (Skit)
- Stop light or picture of stop light (Bible Lesson)

LEADER DEVOTION • • • • •

PSALM 23:4 & PROVERBS 3:1-12.

Ancient shepherds used two basic tools to care for their sheep: the rod and the staff. A rod is a thick club shepherds throw to protect their sheep from themselves and outside predators. For example, if a sheep is headed toward a poisonous plant, a shepherd will expertly throw the rod as a warning to the sheep to stay away from that area. The rod is also used to divide the wool of the sheep, so shepherds can closely check the condition of the sheep's skin. The staff is used to rescue and to guide sheep onto the right path as well as bring individual sheep closer to their shepherd for inspection.

In Psalm 23, these tools comfort the sheep, because they signify another aspect of the Good Shepherd's care: His sovereignty over the sheep. Like the Good Shepherd in Psalm 23, God cares for His children. He loves them, provides for them, guides them, protects them, and corrects them. In Proverbs 3, Solomon urges his children to accept the Lord's correction rather than despise it, because learning from the Lord's correction brings wisdom and life.

It is natural to shy away from correction. Sometimes, we do not want to confront the sin in our hearts, because we know eradicating sin can be a difficult process. We do not want to admit sin exists in our lives, because it's hard to relinquish complete control to the Lord. But God loves us too much to leave us in a state where we are riddled by the pests of sin in our hearts. Confronting the sin in our lives is the act of a loving Shepherd caring for the needs of His sheep. David understood the importance of God's loving correction and actually chose to seek God's inspection in Psalm 139.

"Search me, O God, and know my heart; test me and know my anxious thoughts. Point out anything in me that offends you, and lead me along the path of everlasting life." Psalm 139:23-24

Take time to seek God's correction. Ask Him to identify sin in your life and give you the power to eradicate it. Thank the Lord for His watchful protection over your life, both from outside enemies and the enemy of personal sin.

Pray the kids in your group will begin to understand the great love the Lord has for them. Pray God will make their hearts soft towards Him and His Word.

LESSON 5

PRE-SERVICE

Play a combination of upbeat music and fun video elements before worship begins. Encourage your JUMP Team to welcome kids and engage them in conversation.

COUNTDOWN VIDEO

JUMP Worship is starting! Lead the congregation in counting down. Worshiping together is fun, and we are ready to begin!

SONG

Lead the congregation in a fun worship song.

MAIN POINT VIDEO

WELCOME

Welcome to JUMP, where we worship God together! My name is _____ . I am in charge of JUMP. That means I take care of everyone and everything in this room. If you have a problem, you can talk to me or any of our amazing JUMP Team volunteers. I may be in charge of this room, but there is Someone who is in charge of everything and everyone. Our Main Point today is "The Lord Is in Charge."

(Make motions to help kids understand the Main Point. Repeat the Main Point a few times together before continuing.)

Great job! Before we get started, we have a few rules to help us worship God together. Who remembers rule number one? Rule number one is STAY QUIET. Show me what it should sound like in this room when someone like me is talking. (*Wait for the group to become very quiet.)* You all know exactly what to do. Great job! God has something to say to you and me, and we do not want to miss it. Rule number two is KEEP YOUR HANDS AND FEET TO YOURSELF. Instead of using your hands and feet to bother people, use your hands and feet to worship God. Following this rule will help us focus on God and not on the people around us. Rule number three is STAND DURING SONGS. JUMP is not a show! When you hear a song, stand and worship with us. We want everyone to participate. The last rule is − say it with me - HAVE FUN!

We are going to have so much fun today at J's Diner! Let's get started by talking to God, who is in charge of all things. Everyone bow your heads and close your eyes. We bow our heads to show respect, and we close our eyes to help us focus on God alone.

PRAY

Lead the congregation in prayer.

SONG

Lead the congregation in a fun worship song.

JUMP SKIT

See skit script beginning on page 86.

LESSON 5 SKIT
THE LORD IS IN CHARGE

PIXEL is playing on his phone and UM is reading a menu.

PIXEL: Working at Grandpa's Diner has been epic!

UM: Um, I know! I was just sitting here, memorizing the menu BACKWARDS! I've already memorized it the normal way but now I'm challenging my brain to learn it opposite! Watch this ... SISPU – the Sandwich Ingredient Secret Panini Ummy!

PIXEL: Haaha! That's funny! Let me try! *Takes menu from UM.* Fried chicken with French fries with salt ... salt with fries French with chicken fried! Oh yeah! You've just been Pixilated!

UM: That was AWESOME!

PIXEL: Okay Um, now I need to focus. I'm working on making a new app for my phone. It's this game that involves SUPERHEROES! It's going to be so cool!

SFX: DOOR CHIME

PIXEL: First customer of the day! You know what we gotta do!

SFX: J'S DINER JINGLE

PIXEL and UM begin the jingle they sing whenever a customer comes in. PIXEL begins to sing it and then sees who the customer is and immediately becomes embarrassed.

PIXEL: Cut it out Um! We don't have time for that childish play.

UM: What are you talking about Pixel? We sing that song every time a costumer walks in. That's what we do here at J's Diner!

PIXEL: I just do that, because I know you think it's fun. I've been meaning to tell you I think it's silly.

UM: Whatever Pixel. What's gotten into you?

PIXEL: *Talking to customer, trying to act cool.* Hey man! What's up?

FRIEND: Hey. Do I know you? You look super familiar.

PIXEL: Yeah man, we were in the same biology class last year. Oh, and the same Spanish class, and in Algebra and English ... but whatever man, it's not a big deal that you don't know my name. My name is Pixel. *Goes to high five his friend.*

UM: Um, earth to Pixel! Why do you keep saying "man" and why do you sound like you're trying to make your voice lower? You sound a little kid trying to talk like a big grown up. Hahahaha!

PIXEL: *To Um so friend can't hear.* Stop it Um! That guy is the coolest guy at our school. He is THE football player. Everyone knows him. Just back off so I can talk to my friend like an adult.

UM: Ummm ...

PIXEL: HUSH!

UM: But you're not ...

PIXEL: I said HUSH!

UM: But you're not an adult, Pixel!

PIXEL: ENOUGH!

UM: Hi! I'm Pixel's younger sibling. My name is Um, like the letters U and M. It's a nickname my brother gave me when I was little because I'd say "ummmm this" and "ummmm that" ... Anyway, what's your name?!

PIXEL: Stop it, Um. He's an adult, just like me. He doesn't have time to make chit chat with a little rascal like you. Could I get you a menu?

FRIEND: That'd be great. I've heard great things about this place!

PIXEL: You've heard about us?!?! I mean ... yeah, man ... here it is.

Friend begins to read menu.

GRANDPA J: Well, hey hey hey! It's a great day with Grandpa J! Looks like your buddy from school is here! Isn't he the quarterback on your football team? How ya doing partner? Great to see ya in J's Diner today!

Friend waves at camera.

GRANDPA J: Now Pixel, Make sure you tell them about the UPSIS Combo. It's only $5.99 for the entire meal – UPSIS, fries and a drink! Now that's a bargain if I ever saw one!! Bye kiddos!

Grandpa J Video 1 ends

UM: *To friend.* That's our Grandpa J! He owns the diner! He's out of town right now so he put us in charge of running the diner and getting more customers to know about how AWESOME it is! Just like real adults.

PIXEL: Stop it Um. We're having cool adult talk right now.

UM: Ya'll aren't adults! And you're definitely not cool.

PIXEL: For real Um, just go away. Why don't you go make the meal for my friend?

UM: Well okay! What would you like?

FRIEND: That special your grandpa was talking about sounds great! Can I get that meal?

UM: Sure! One UPSIS COMBO coming right up! *Um exits.*

PIXEL: The UPSIS has been getting us all new customers in here lately! It's pretty cool. Kinda like football. Football is cool, too.

FRIEND: Yeah. I love playing football. I'm looking forward to all our games this season. What do you think about the new running back? Think he's going to be a pass first or rush first?

PIXEL: *Hesitating with response, unsure of the answer.* He'll be a solid combination of both. I've got a fantasy football team.

FRIEND: Do you play actual football … ?

PIXEL: Well, sorta ... I mean ... I ....

UM enters with brown bag with "combo" inside.

UM: ONE UPSIS COMBO at your service!

FRIEND: Awesome, thanks so much!

UM begins to exit but hides under the table.

FRIEND: Here ya go! *Starts to hand PIXEL money.*

PIXEL: Hey man, no worries. You can have that for free.

FRIEND: Are you sure? I know your grandpa said that the meal was $5.99.

PIXEL: Yeah, but I don't really listen to him. I'm really the one in charge around here.

FRIEND: You are? Aren't you like, 17 years old?? I mean ... We go to school together ...

PIXEL: Well, yes ... But Grandpa J's not here ... So, I'm in charge.

FRIEND: Did he tell you that?

PIXEL: Well ... Nooo, but don't worry about it. Just enjoy the meal for free.

FRIEND: Awesome dude. Thanks so much! Let's play football sometime!

PIXEL: Totally man! That would be awesome! *Trying to contain his excitement.*

Friend begins to exit with meal.

FRIEND: Bye guys!

PIXEL: Ahhh! NO WAY!!! He and I are pretty much best friends now. Coolest. Day. Ever!

UM pops up and scares PIXEL.

UM: Hi.

PIXEL: *Girly scream* Ahhh!! I mean *low pitched* Ahhhhh! Where did you come from?

UM: Well, I just wanted to hear your conversation. He seemed like a pretty cool guy.

PIXEL: First off, you were eaves dropping. Second off, he IS a cool guy.

UM: Earth to Pixel, you didn't have him pay!! YOU AREN'T ALLOWED TO DO THAT!!

PIXEL: Yeah, well... It's not a big deal

UM: What?!?!?? You can't do that! Every customer has to pay! That's the rule! Grandpa J is in charge, and that's what he said!

PIXEL: Listen, Um. That was like the coolest guy at school. I just needed to do that. It's adult stuff.

UM: You're not an adult!! Plus, no matter how old we are, we have to listen to the one in charge! You know, what you did just now is considered stealing. You would never want to steal from Grandpa J or hurt Grandpa J with your actions.

PIXEL: Well, I didn't think of it as stealing ....

Grandpa J Video 2

> **GRANDPA J:** Well, hey hey hey! It's a great day with Grandpa J! How's it going down there?

UM and PIXEL stay quiet.

> **GRANDPA J:** Well, hey hey hey! It's a great day with Grandpa J! How's it going down there?

UM and PIXEL stay quiet.

> **GRANDPA J:** UM! PIXEL! WHAT IS GOING ON?

UM: Pixel gave a free meal to his friend and said that he doesn't care that you're in charge!

PIXEL: UM!!!!!

> **GRANDPA J:** Pixel, is that true?

PIXEL: Yes....

GRANDPA J: Pixel, you know the rules. You know that I'm in charge. You must have every customer pay. No matter who they are. That's part of working at the diner. You make amazing food. You serve the food. You take the money. And thank the customer.

PIXEL: I'm really sorry...

GRANDPA J: But more importantly, Pixel, you clearly know I'm in charge of the diner and you disobeyed the rules. And even more importantly, your actions hurt me. It hurts me that you did not follow the rules and were disobedient. Now I'm here to shepherd you, to guide you, while you work at the diner. So as your shepherd, I must help fix your actions when they need correction. I want you to realize I love you and I care for you. As your Grandpa, I also want the best for you. You know, this is just how God cares for us. The Lord cares for us. He uses the rod and staff as a form of correction. Just like the Lord guides us to the right path, it's my job to guide you on the right path. Can you two say, "The Lord Is In Charge."

PIXEL & UM: The Lord Is in Charge.

GRANDPA J: Now Pixel, I'm going to have to give you a consequence for your action. I'm going to need you to pay back the money owed to the diner for that meal, and to help you remember to do the right thing, I'd like you to not play on your phone for the next 3 days. This is the consequence for your actions. No playing on your cell phone.

PIXEL: I understand.

GRANDPA J: Pixel, I want you to know I love you. And because I love you, I want to make sure you are walking along the path of righteousness and making good choices. Love you, buddy.

PIXEL: Thanks, Grandpa. Love you too. Bye!

Grandpa J Video 2 ends.

UM: Sorry I tattled on you, Pixel ... I didn't mean to get you in trouble. Sometimes words just come out of my mouth and then I can't NOT tell the truth and then I start babbling on and on and on and don't even realize it ...

PIXEL: *Cutting Um off.* Actually Um, I'm glad you told Grandpa J. I needed to be reminded Grandpa is in charge. And more importantly, God is in charge. He wants the best for us.

UM: Hey … I know! How about we play some football …? You don't get to play on your phone for the next 3 days, so we could definitely get some great practice in for football season!

PIXEL: Okay Um! Great idea! Okay here it goes …. Go long! *Throws a football. Um runs off stage and we hear a crash.*

SFX: CRASH

UM: *From offstage* I'm okay!

GAME VIDEO

SONG   *Lead the congregation in a fun worship song.*

BIBLE LESSON

BIBLE LESSON INTRO VIDEO

 INTRO

Have any of you ever gotten in trouble for doing something wrong? I know I have! Why do you think our parents punish us when we do something wrong? Our parents punish us, because they love us! *(Tell a personal story about a time when you did something wrong as a child and were punished. Tell what you learned from that punishment.)*

Imagine what kind of person you would be as an adult if your parents never corrected you. What kind of person would you grow up to be if they allowed you to be mean to your brothers and sisters, throw temper tantrums to get your way, and lie to everyone. You would not be a fun person to be around! We need our parents, teachers, and other authorities to be in charge. We need them to help us learn how to grow up into godly men and women. Today's Bible lesson is about Psalm 23:4b, where David tells us the Good Shepherd is in charge.

 READ THE BIBLE

Read Psalm 23:1-4.

David, the author of this psalm, is so glad to have a Good Shepherd! During this song, David brags on God, his Good Shepherd. God loves him, provides for him, guides him, and even protects him from danger. In the last part of verse 4, David brags on God for something you might think is strange. David says the shepherd's rod and staff comfort him. A rod and staff are tools that shepherds use to protect, guide, and discipline their sheep.

Make or bring a shepherd's staff and a thick club-like stick to represent the rod. Hold these objects as you teach. Demonstrate how the shepherd would use each item. For added effect, use a JUMP Team Member volunteer as the sheep.

Shepherds use the staff to keep sheep from straying away from the good grazing fields. The staff is also used to bring individual sheep close to the shepherd, so the shepherd can inspect the sheep for bugs and pests.

The rod is one of the tools shepherds use to defend against predators. They practice regularly to be sure their aim is very good. If a predator starts to stalk a sheep, a good shepherd will expertly throw the rod at the predator, scaring it away. Sometimes, a shepherd will throw the rod at or near his own sheep to keep them from eating poisonous plants or being mean to other sheep.

You might wonder why these tools, the rod and staff, would comfort a sheep. After all, why would the sheep like being hooked around the neck by the shepherd's staff or having a rod thrown at the food they were about to eat? Sheep find the staff comforting, because they would rather be hooked by the staff than be lost from their shepherd! The sheep would rather be hit with the shepherd's rod than unknowingly eat poisonous weeds! The shepherd is in charge and will protect them, even from themselves. Knowing that the shepherd is in charge allows the sheep to live without fear.

In the same way, when we choose to put Jesus in charge of our lives, He will protect us, even from ourselves, so we can live without fear.

Read Proverbs 3:5-6.

How many of you have heard that you are supposed to "be true to your heart" or "follow your heart?" Lots of people think the best way to get through life is just to do whatever you want. But the Bible tells us about another way. Proverbs 3:5-6 tells us to trust God's way instead of our own. God wants us to follow Him first, not our hearts. We will want different things through life, and that's okay. But we should always follow God first, asking Him what He wants us to do.

Of course, we don't always get it right. Even the nicest people, the most famous pastors, and greatest parents make mistakes. We choose to sin, to do things that we know are wrong. When we sin, there are consequences.

Sometimes, we get angry and blame other people for what we did wrong. Why do I have to be grounded?! Why should I have to do my brother's chores for a week?! What I did wasn't that bad. It's really someone else's fault!

However, the purpose of punishment is for us to repent, learn, and grow.

Read Proverbs 3:11-12.

When someone gives us a punishment for the wrong things we have done, God wants us to remember that He loves us. Punishment is for our protection. Punishment helps us learn to live God's way.

OBJECT LESSON

So how should we react to God's correction? When you do something wrong, remember a stoplight.

1. **RED LIGHT – STOP.** Stop what you were (or are) doing wrong right away. Ask for forgiveness.

2. **YELLOW LIGHT – THINK.** What can you do to keep from making the same mistake again?

3. **GREEN LIGHT – GO.** Keep going! Start living for God again, knowing He has forgiven you and loves you very much.

APPLICATION

Remember that God is in charge. He corrects us for good reasons. The next time you sin, listen to God's correction. Stop and ask for forgiveness, think about how you can keep from doing it again, and go on living for God!

PRAY

We are now going into our time of offering. "Offering" is a big word for present. This is the time when we give our presents to the Lord, our Shepherd. We give back to God from everything He has given to us. Let's stand together and sing this song as an offering, a big present to God.

OFFERING SONG

Lead the congregation in a slower worship song.

PRAY

Lead the congregation in prayer.

MEMORY VERSE VIDEO

MEMORY VERSE

Are you ready to memorize Psalm 23? I know I am! First let's review what we have learned already. Remember, we sing the word "Psalm", because Psalms is a book of songs. *(Review the verses using the motions you used in the previous lessons.)*

Repeat after me:
Psaaaaalm 23. *(Psaaaaalm 23)*
The Lord is my shepherd. I shall not want. *(The Lord is my shepherd. I shall not want.)*
He makes me lie down in green pastures. *(He makes me lie down in green pastures.)*
He leads me beside quiet waters. *(He leads me beside quiet waters.)*
He guides me in the paths of righteousness *(He guides me in the paths of righteousness)*
For His name's sake. *(For His name's sake.)*
Even though I walk through the valley of the shadow of death, *(Even though I walk through the valley of the shadow of death,)*
I fear no evil, for You are with me. *(I fear no evil, for You are with me.)*

Great job! The next part of Psalm 23 says, "Your rod and Your staff, they comfort me." Can you imagine what would happen to a lamb if its shepherd never corrected it? That poor lamb would eat poisonous plants and walk right into danger! Thankfully we serve a God who loves us very much. He corrects us when we are wrong and teaches us to live His righteous, right way.

(Ask kids to give suggestions for motions to this part of the verse. Once you have decided on the motions, repeat verse 4b once together. Then say the verses together.)

Great job! Now let's say it all together, starting with "Psaaaaalm 23." Three, two, one –

Psaaaaalm 23. The Lord is my shepherd, I shall not want.
He makes me lie down in green pastures
He leads me beside quiet waters.
He restores my soul;
He guides me in paths of righteousness for His name's sake.
Even though I walk through the valley of the shadow of death,
I fear no evil, for You are with me;
Your rod and Your staff, they comfort me.

Great job! Do you think you can say this much without looking at the screens? I think you can! *(Remove the verse from the screens. Let kids lead you in reciting the verses.)* You are all so smart. Way to go!

SONG

Lead the congregation in a fun worship song.

ANNOUNCEMENTS

Use this time to encourage kids to bring friends and participate in whatever you may have coming up next.

REVIEW GAME

It's time for the REVIEW GAME!! I need one volunteer from each grade to come up on stage. I will choose people who have been listening and paying attention the whole service and want to play in our game.

Choose contestants and introduce them to the group in game show style.

During this game, your grade can win by getting very quiet when you hear the wrong answer and very loud when you hear the right answer. Each grade is going to have a different silly move and sound that you must do when you think you hear the right answer. *(Let your contestants choose a silly motion and sound for their grade.)*

I hope you are ready. I hope you have been paying attention, because the game begins ... NOW!

Give kids the opportunity to do their motions and silly sounds when they hear the correct answer. Award points to the grade who is the quietest when they hear the wrong answer and participates the most when they hear the right answer.

Question 1. What is our Main Point today?
a. The Lord Is My Shepherd.
b. The Lord Is in Charge.
c. The Lord Doesn't Care and Lets Me Do Whatever I Want.
d. Staffs Look Like Upside-down Candy Canes.

Question 2. Where can you find today's Bible lesson?
a. Jonah 23
b. John 23
c. Psalm 23
d. Jude 23

Question 3. Who wrote Psalm 23?
a. David
b. Jonathon
c. Peter
d. A baby goat

Option: Find a short video clip of a baby goat screaming online. Play this short clip every time you use "baby goat" as a choice. Act surprised and confused every time it plays. Let the kids laugh, then repeat the question again.

Question 4: Psalm 23:4b says, "Your rod and your staff, they _____."
a. scare me
b. help me
c. comfort me
d. are super awesome

Question 5: Psalm 23:4a says, "Even though I walk through the valley of _____, I fear no evil, for You are with me."
a. shenanigans
b. the shadow of baby goats
c. the shadow of wolves
d. the shadow of death

Question 6: Psalm 23:3 says, "He restores my soul; He guides me in the _____ for His name's sake."
a. paths of righteousness
b. paths of ripe bananas
c. paths with lots of people
d. paths of baby goats

Question 7: Psalm 23:2 says, "He makes me lie down in green pastures. He leads me beside _____."

    a. quiet pastors

    b. quiet waters

    c. stormy waters

    d. baby goats

SONG

Lead the congregation in a fun worship song.

DISMISSAL

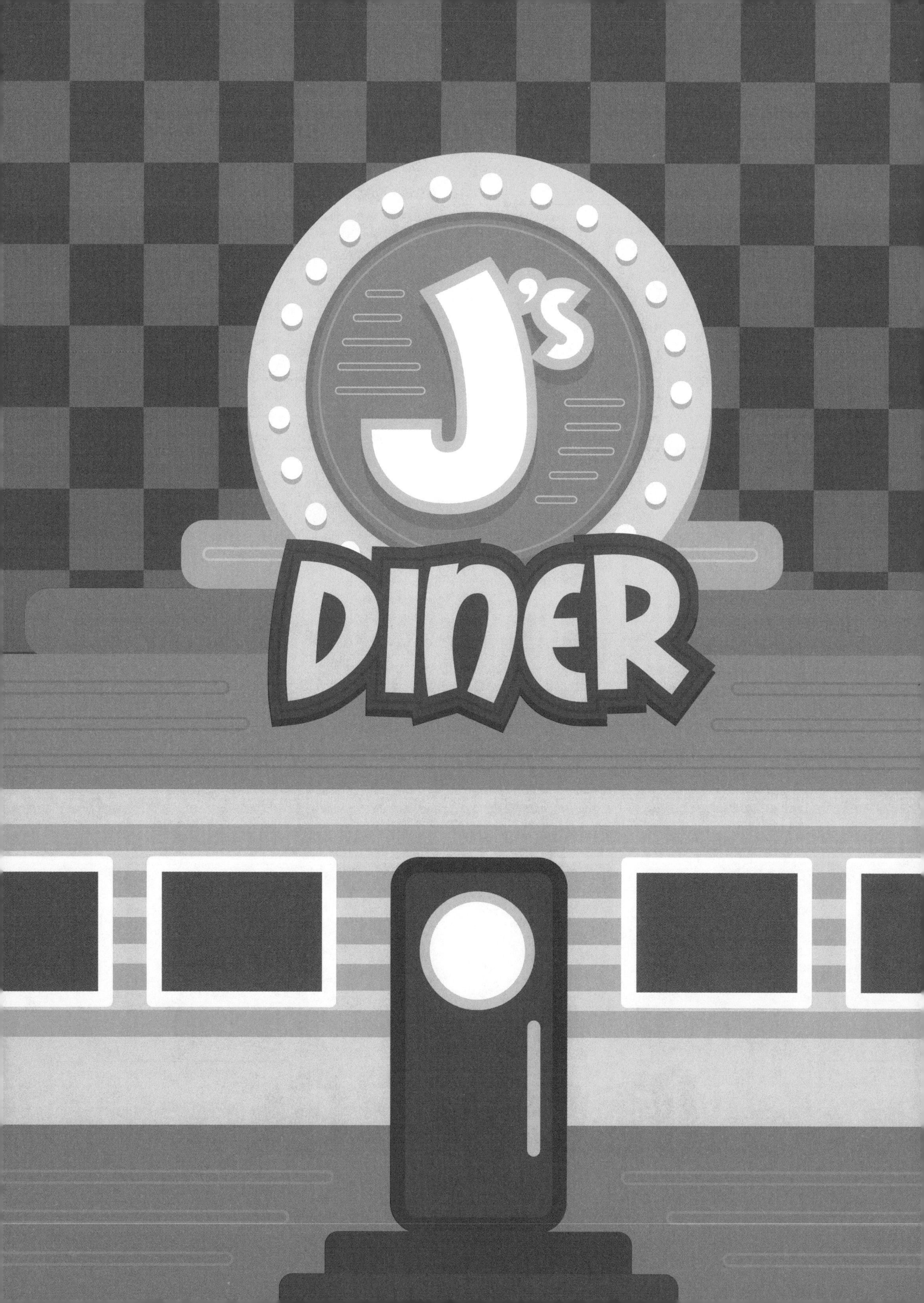
J's
DINER

LESSON 6

JUMP WORSHIP

MAIN POINT The Lord Prepares the Way for Me.

SCRIPTURE Psalm 23:5; John 14:1-6;
Ephesians 2:8-10; 1 Corinthians 10:13

MEMORY VERSE Psalm 23

"The Lord is my shepherd, I shall not want.
He makes me lie down in green pastures;
He leads me beside quiet waters.
He restores my soul; He guides me in the paths of
righteousness for His name's sake.
Even though I walk through the valley of the shadow of death,
I fear no evil, for You are with me;
Your rod and Your staff, they comfort me.
You prepare a table before me in the presence of my enemies;
You have anointed my head with oil; My cup overflows.
Surely goodness and lovingkindness will follow me all the
days of my life, and I will dwell in the house of the Lord forever."

TODAY'S SPECIAL

PSALM 23:5

THE PANTRY

LESSON 6

OVERVIEW

SPIRITUAL CONNECTION:

Pixel and Um use the Manager's Manual to help the customers in J's Diner. Grandpa J gave solutions to even the craziest of problems in the Manager's Manual. Because Grandpa J prepared the solutions beforehand, Pixel and Um were able to solve each customer's problem. In Psalm 23, we learn the Lord prepares a way for us to heaven through His son Jesus Christ. Jesus has taken care of all our needs and will continue to take care of us in every situation.

CHARACTERS:

PIXEL - Tech savy, music loving, older brother of Um

UM - Talkative, story-telling, fun-loving, younger sister of Pixel

CUSTOMER 1 - Upset customer who spilled a drink in their car

CUSTOMER 2 - Upset customer who has a brain freeze

CUSTOMER 3 - Upset customer with monkeys in their car

COSTUMES:

PIXEL - Orange shirt, jeans, white apron, and diner hat

UM - Purple shirt, jeans, white apron, and diner hat

CUSTOMER 1 - Everyday clothes, wet from a spilled drink

CUSTOMER 2 - Everyday clothes with a jacket and other cold weather accessories

CUSTOMER 3 - Everyday clothes, disheveled

PROPS:

- White spray bottle (Skit)
- Manager manual (Skit)
- Can of powder (Skit)
- Paper (Bible Lesson)

LEADER DEVOTION

READ PSALM 23:5, JOHN 14:1-6, EPHESIANS 2:8-10, & 1 CORINTHIANS 10:13.

The "table" in Psalm 23:5 most likely refers to the tablelands, or mesas, where shepherds take their sheep for the summer season. Shepherds make the journey to the high plateaus many times before taking their flock to prepare the land for grazing. They add salt and minerals to the fields, pluck out poisonous plants, and deal with any other problems they might encounter. The shepherd goes ahead of his flock to prepare a place for them.

Christ, our Good Shepherd, has gone ahead of us, too. He has prepared a way for us to get to Heaven, a place for us in Heaven, and good works for us to do while we are still on earth. God has prepared everything we need to follow Him – even a way out when we are faced with the temptation to sin.

Once again, Psalm 23 reminds Christians that nothing surprises God. He has gone ahead of us in life to prepare the way for us. He has prepared the good times and the bad times. He has prepared our circumstances, and He has prepared our hearts to live abundantly in every situation we may face.

When you are tempted to sin, take a moment to reflect on the fact that Jesus has gone before you, preparing you for this moment in your life. Thank Him for going ahead of you and look for opportunities to do the good He has planned for you in every situation.

As you prepare, pray for the kids and families represented in your group. Ask God to prepare their hearts to hear the Good News that Jesus Christ has prepared the way for them.

PRE-SERVICE

Play a combination of upbeat music and fun video elements before worship begins. Encourage your JUMP Team to welcome kids and engage them in conversation.

COUNTDOWN VIDEO

JUMP Worship is starting! Lead the congregation in counting down. Worshiping together is fun, and we are ready to begin!

SONG

Lead the congregation in a fun worship song.

MAIN POINT VIDEO

WELCOME

Welcome to JUMP, where we worship God together! My name is _____ . I am so excited to worship with you today. Did you know lots of people have worked very hard to prepare for worship today? *(Commend the volunteers and staff who help prepare for children's worship consistently. Point out specific ways they prepare for the kids to worship.)* Today we are going to learn about the ways Jesus prepares the way for us. Our Main Point today is "The Lord Prepares the Way for Me."

(Make motions to help kids understand the Main Point. Repeat the Main Point a few times together before continuing.)

Great job! Before we get started, we have a few rules to help us worship God together. Who remembers rule number one? Rule number one is STAY QUIET. God has something to say to you and me, and we do not want to miss it. Rule number two is KEEP YOUR HANDS AND FEET TO YOURSELF. Instead of using your hands and feet to bother people, use your hands and feet to worship God. Following this rule will help us focus on God and not on the people around us. Rule number three is STAND DURING SONGS. JUMP is not a show! When you hear a song, stand and worship with us. We want everyone to participate. The last rule is – say it with me - HAVE FUN!

We are going to have so much fun today at J's Diner! Let's get started by talking to the Lord in prayer. Everyone bow your heads and close your eyes. We bow our heads to show respect, and we close our eyes to help us focus on God alone.

PRAY

Lead the congregation in prayer.

SONG

Lead the congregation in a fun worship song.

JUMP SKIT

See skit script beginning on page 106.

LESSON 6 SKIT
THE LORD PREPARES A WAY FOR ME

Skit Intro Video

Grandpa J Video 1

GRANDPA J: Well, hey hey hey! It's a great day with Grandpa J! You guys have been outstanding this summer! You have earned your spot. You have worked hard, learned some hard lessons and made our diner a hip and happening place! I want to promote you both to managers here at the Diner!

UM & PIXEL: MANAGERS?! AWESOME!!

GRANDPA J: Now, all you need to do is study the Manager's Manual. The manual has the solution to any problem that might arise while you are working here. I need you both to study, read and memorize that information. It will help you when you find yourself in a heap of trouble. Bye now kiddos!

Grandpa J Video 1 ends

PIXEL and UM get excited.

UM: *Singing.* We're going to be managers! We're going to be managers!

PIXEL: I know I know! But we need to start studying that manual.

PIXEL grabs the manual from behind the counter and sits down to start studying. UM doesn't realize he has the manual.

UM: Ummm ... Right! I wonder where that manual is ... If you were the Manager Manual, where would you be hiding? I know! I'll bet it's over here! *Runs offstage.* Not there, maybe over here! *Runs other way off stage.* Nope not there either ... Manual, manual, manual ... Oh where are you???

PIXEL: Earth to UM! *Shows manual in hand.*

UM: BAH! Right! Lets get studying!

SFX: DOOR CHIME

PIXEL: We've got our first customer of the day! You know what it's time for....

SFX: J'S DINER JINGLE

CUSTOMER 1: Hi there! Is there a manager I can speak with?

PIXEL: Well, well, well, I'm glad you asked! Manager Pixel at your service! How can I help?!?

CUSTOMER 1: I went through the drive through and the lid popped off my drink and spilled all over my car. How do I clean it?

PIXEL: Well, it looks like we've got our first issue as OFFICIAL MANAGERS!

SFX: EPIC

UM: No worries! We've got this manual that tells us what to do! Let's just see if there's a solution for cleaning your spilled drink!

Manual Video 1

To clean a spilled drink: Check the supplies in the cleaning cabinet. There is spill-no-more solution in a white bottle. Spray that three times and liquid should disappear and your spill will be no more!

UM: WOW! I'm so impressed Grandpa knew to put these instructions in the manual.

CUSTOMER 1: Let's give it a shot!

All exit.

Later Slide

All enter.

CUSTOMER 1: Wow! It's like a bottle of magic.

PIXEL: Grandpa J to the rescue!

CUSTOMER 1: Thanks! Bye! *Exits.*

UM: I'm so impressed Grandpa J had the SOLUTION to the problem. This manual just might come in handy.

CUSTOMER 2 enters.   **SFX: DOOR CHIME**

PIXEL: UM! Wow! Another customer already??? It's like Black Friday in here! Let's do what we do best ....

SFX: J'S DINER JINGLE

CUSTOMER 2: I drank my ice-UPSIS-popsicle too fast and got a brain freeze!

UM: Ummm ... A brain freeze?! I know just how to stop a brain freeze!

PIXEL: You do?

UM: Yes! You jump on your left foot three times and then spin around in a circle with your tongue out and then squeal like a dolphin *They all three do it.*

CUSTOMER 2: It didn't work!!!

PIXEL: Why don't we just check the manual? Let's see.... Brain freeze starts with the letter "B" ... Balloon floats away? No ... Baboons take my lunch money? No ... Bear ate my birthday cake? Oh here it is! Brain freeze!

Manual Video 2

If a brain freeze occurs, then place your thumb on the roof of your mouth for 3 seconds.

CUSTOMER 2 does as it says as all freeze on stage.

LATER SLIDE

CUSTOMER 2: It worked!!! Wow! Thanks so much! You two are quite the managers! I'm very impressed!

UM: Thank ya, thank ya! Just call me manager UMMMMMMMMM!

CUSTOMER 2: Are you thinking?

UM: No! My name is Manager UMMMMMMM!

CUSTOMER 2: Is there something you needed to say?

UM: No no no! It's my name! My name is UM!

CUSTOMER 2: Oh …. I get it … Kinda … Well Um, thanks again!

CUSTOMER 2 exits.

CUSTOMER 3 enters.   **SFX: DOOR CHIME**

PIXEL: What?! Another customer already!!!! You'd think we just released the new iPhone!!!

SFX: J'S DINER JINGLE

CUSTOMER 3: Hello there kids. I need some help. You see, I ordered a banana milkshake and then a brigade of monkeys smelled the bananas and came barging into my car to drink it all!

PIXEL: Wow! That sounds quite unique. I really don't know what to do in this situation.

UM: Ummm, Pixel. Remember. Grandpa said to use the manual.

PIXEL: I highly doubt grandpa put instructions about this in the manual.

UM: Just like you said earlier, nothing surprises Grandpa. Let's just look in the manual! Look! It says it right here!

Manual Video 3

> If a brigade of monkeys enter your car, use the monkey-be-gone powder. It's in the cleaning supplies closet. Just pour some powder on the ground and they'll fall asleep and dream of lollipops made of bananas!

UM: Wow! Grandpa really has thought of everything!

PIXEL: Nothing surprises Grandpa! He has prepared our way for us as managers and we can trust him to guide us!

UM: Here you go, nice customer with a brigade of monkeys in your car … Try this powder.

CUSTOMER 3 exits.

LATER Slide

CUSTOMER 3 enters.

CUSTOMER 3: It worked! The monkeys are fast asleep and dreaming of lollipops made of bananas! Thanks so much! You are two of the finest managers I've ever seen!

PIXEL & UM: Thanks!

CUSTOMER 3 exits.

UM: Wow, Grandpa really prepared the way for us!

Grandpa Video 2

> **GRANDPA J:** Well, hey hey hey! It's a great day with Grandpa J! How are my two favorite managers doing?

UM & PIXEL: Great!!

> **GRANDPA J:** Glad to hear it! Is the Manager Manual coming in handy?

UM: Yes!!! You have thought of everything Grandpa J!!! We are so thankful for this manual!

> **GRANDPA J:** I'd like to think I've covered the bases of being a manager. But you know, just like I prepared the Manager Manual for you to use, God has prepared a way for us to Heaven through His Son Jesus Christ. Jesus has taken care of all our needs and will continue to take care of us in every situation. The Lord prepares the way for me. Can you say that?

UM & PIXEL: The Lord prepares the way for me!

> **GRANDPA J:** That's right. Now, you two keep studying that manual ... Looks like you might have a pretty busy day! Bye!

Grandpa Video 2 ends

UM: Grandpa J really did prepare everything we needed! Let's get to memorizing!

Both exit.

GAME VIDEO

SONG *Lead the congregation in a fun worship song.*

BIBLE LESSON

BIBLE LESSON INTRO VIDEO

 ### INTRO

How many of you have ever tried to put something together without the instructions? Toy blocks, furniture, and other building projects can be very difficult. When you look at all the tiny blocks that are supposed to build that giant spaceship, airplane, or police station, it seems like one big mess. It's just a big pile of blocks with matching colors, and it can be hard to see the big picture of what you are building.

That's why almost all building kits come with a picture of the finished product. That picture is proof someone has built something amazing using the same pieces that you have in front of you. If you follow the instructions provided in the box or online, you can build that same thing, too. The picture on the box is a guarantee. Someone has done this before you, and it worked. You can do it, too.

Today, we are going to learn that **the Lord prepares the way for us**. He sees all of the pieces of our lives and knows exactly how they all fit together. Like the people who make the pictures on the boxes, Jesus has gone ahead of us, preparing the way for us in life.

 ## READ THE BIBLE

Read Psalm 23:1-5.

In Psalm 23, David tells us that the good shepherd goes ahead of his flock, preparing the way for his sheep. The "table" in this verse refers to the "tablelands," high places sheep went during the winter months to graze. Shepherds went to these high plateaus to prepare the fields for grazing by planting good seed, removing poisonous weeds, and monitoring any potential predators. When the sheep arrived at the table, the shepherd had already done all of the hard work! All the sheep had to do was enjoy.

Jesus, our Good Shepherd, has prepared the way for us, too. He has prepared the way to Heaven, good things for us to do while we are still on earth, and a way out of every temptation to sin.

OBJECT LESSON

Search "paper airplane object lesson" on YouTube for specific instructions.

John 14:6 tells us Jesus made the only way for us to get to Heaven. Accepting Jesus' forgiveness and choosing to put Him in charge of your life is the only way to have a forever friendship with God and a forever home with Him in Heaven.

Ephesians 2:10 tells us God has prepared good works for us to do while we are on earth, so be on the look out! Look for opportunities to do good things for the people God loves: everyone!

1 Corinthians 10:13 tells us Jesus has also provided a way out of every temptation to sin that will ever come our way. When we have Jesus in our lives, we have the power to say NO to sin and YES to Him!

APPLICATION

Our road sign for today says "Under Construction." We may not be able to see the big picture of our lives, but we can trust that God wants to build us into something good. He sees the big picture. God is never surprised by the things that happen. He is in control. He has been there before and is ready for anything that life may bring.

In every situation, Jesus has gone before us. That is a great thing!! We do not need to worry!! **As Psalm 23:5 says, "… My cup overflows."** God has given us more than we need. We can be more than content, knowing Jesus loves us and has made a way for us to live for Him both on earth and in Heaven!

PRAY

We are now going into our time of offering. "Offering" is a big word for present. This is the time when we give our presents to the Lord, our Shepherd. We give back to God from everything He has given to us. Let's stand together and sing this song as an offering, a big present to God.

OFFERING SONG

Lead the congregation in a slower worship song.

PRAY

Lead the congregation in prayer.

MEMORY VERSE VIDEO

MEMORY VERSE

Are you ready to memorize Psalm 23? I know I am! First let's review what we have learned already. Remember, we sing the word "Psalm", because Psalms is a book of songs. (Review the verses using the motions you used in the previous lessons.)

Repeat after me:
Psaaaaalm 23. (Psaaaaalm 23)
The Lord is my shepherd. I shall not want. (The Lord is my shepherd. I shall not want.)
He makes me lie down in green pastures. (He makes me lie down in green pastures.)
He leads me beside quiet waters. (He leads me beside quiet waters.)
He guides me in the paths of righteousness (He guides me in the paths of righteousness)
For His name's sake. (For His name's sake.)
Even though I walk through the valley of the shadow of death, (Even though I walk through the valley of the shadow of death,)
I fear no evil, for You are with me. (I fear no evil, for You are with me.)
Your rod and Your staff, they comfort me. (Your rod and Your staff, they comfort me.)

Great job! The next part of Psalm 23 says, "You prepare a table before me in the presence of my enemies; You have anointed my head with oil; My cup overflows."

This verse is a little longer than the last few, but I know we can do it!
(Ask kids to give suggestions for motions to the key phrases in the verse. Once you have decided on the motions, repeat verse 5 once together.)

Repeat after me:
You prepare a table before me (You prepare a table before me)

in the presence of my enemies; *(in the presence of my enemies;)*
You have anointed my head with oil; *(You have anointed my head with oil;)*
My cup overflows. *(My cup overflows.)*

Now let's put it all together! You can do this! Remember, we sing the word "Psalm" to remind us Psalms is a book of songs. Ready, set, go!

Psaaaaalm 23. The Lord is my shepherd, I shall not want.
He makes me lie down in green pastures
He leads me beside quiet waters.
He restores my soul;
He guides me in paths of righteousness for His name's sake.
Even though I walk through the valley of the shadow of death,
I fear no evil, for You are with me;
Your rod and Your staff, they comfort me.
You prepare a table before me in the presence of my enemies;
You have anointed my head with oil; My cup overflows.

Great job! Do you think you can say this without looking at the screens?
I think you can! *(Remove the verse from the screens. Let kids lead you in reciting the verses.)* We only have one verse left to memorize before we have an entire chapter in the Bible memorized. You are amazing!

SONG

Lead the congregation in a fun worship song.

ANNOUNCEMENTS

Use this time to encourage kids to bring friends and participate in whatever you may have coming up next.

REVIEW GAME

It's time for the REVIEW GAME!! I need one volunteer from each grade to come up on stage. I will choose people who have been listening and paying attention the whole service and want to play in our game.

Choose contestants and introduce them to the group in game show style.

During this game, your grade can win by getting very quiet when you hear the wrong answer and very loud when you hear the right answer. Each grade is going to have a different silly move and sound that you must do when you think you hear the right answer. *(Let your contestants choose a silly motion and sound for their grade.)*

I hope you are ready. I hope you have been paying attention, because the game begins ... NOW!

Give kids the opportunity to do their motions and silly sounds when they hear the correct answer. Award points to the grade who is the quietest when they hear the wrong answer and participates the most when they hear the right answer.

Question 1. What is our Main Point today?
    a. The Lord Prepares a Meal for Me.   c. The Llama Prepares to Make a Mini Me.
    b. The Lord Prepares the Way for Me.   d. Everyone Needs a Manager's Manual.

Question 2. Where can you find today's Bible lesson?
    a. Manual 23   **c. Psalm 23**
    b. Matthew 23   d. Malachi 23

Question 3. Who wrote Psalm 23?
    a. David   c. Peter
    b. Jonathon   d. A baby goat

Option: Find a short video clip of a baby goat screaming online. Play this short clip every time you use "baby goat" as a choice. Act surprised and confused every time it plays. Let the kids laugh, then repeat the question again.

Question 4: Psalm 23:5a says, "You prepare a table before me in the presence of my _____."
    a. frienemies   c. sea anemones
    b. enemies   d. mommy

Question 5: Psalm 23:5b says, "You have anointed my head with _____; My cup overflows."
    a. oil   c. Gatorade™
    b. conditioner   d. hair

Question 6: Psalm 23:4b says, "Your rod and your staff, they _____."

a. scare me

c. **comfort me**

b. help me

d. are super awesome

Question 7: Psalm 23:4a says, "Even though I walk through the valley of _____, I fear no evil, for You are with me."

a. shenanigans

c. the shadow of wolves

b. the shadow of baby goats

d. **the shadow of death**

SONG

Lead the congregation in a fun worship song.

DISMISSAL

THE LORD
PREPARES
THE WAY FOR ME

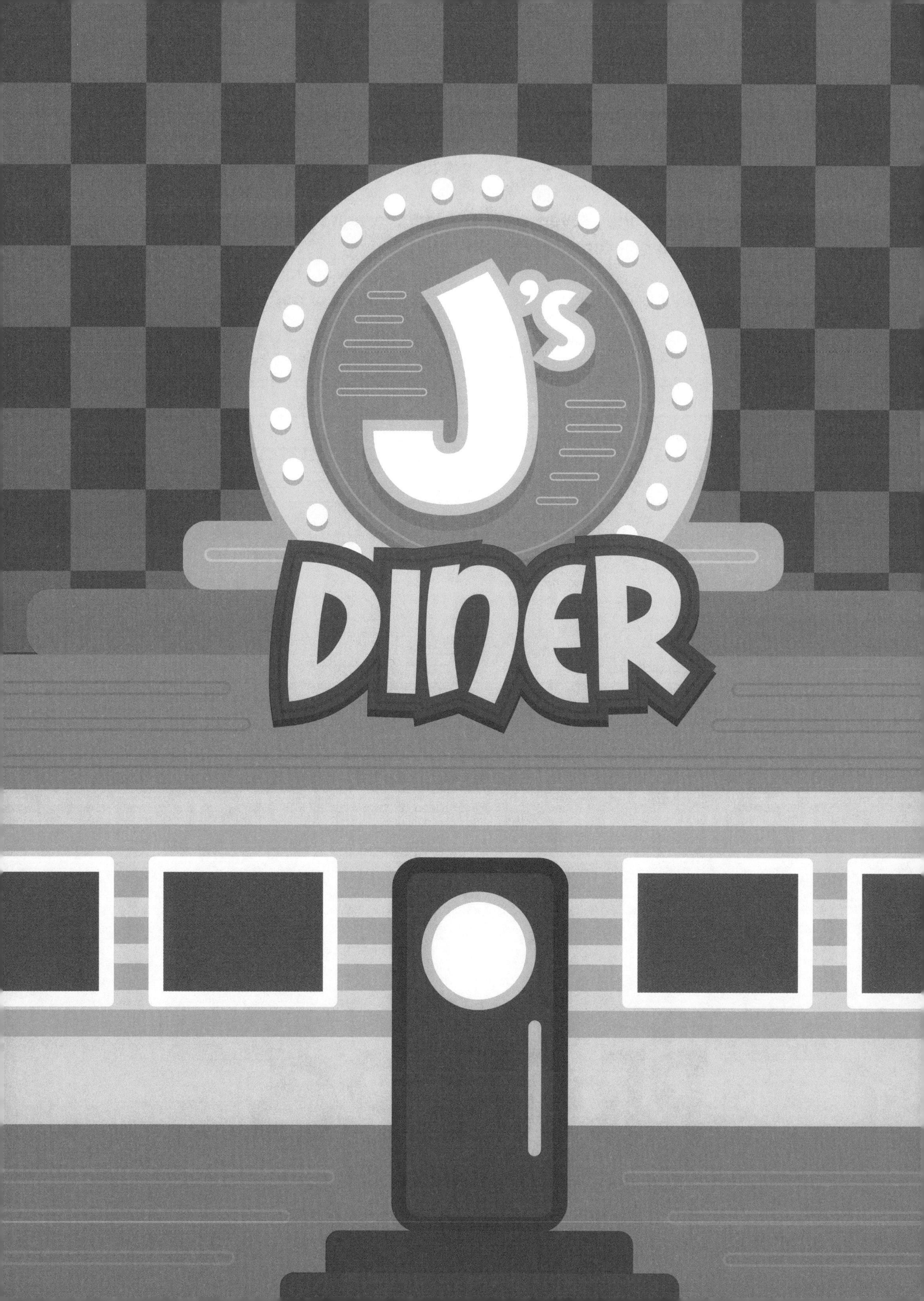
J's
DINER

LESSON 7

MAIN POINT The Lord Gives Me a Forever Home.

SCRIPTURE Psalm 23:6; Philippians 3:17-20; Revelation 21:1-8

MEMORY VERSE Psalm 23

"The Lord is my shepherd, I shall not want.
He makes me lie down in green pastures;
He leads me beside quiet waters.
He restores my soul; He guides me in the paths of
righteousness for His name's sake.
Even though I walk through the valley of the shadow of death,
I fear no evil, for You are with me;
Your rod and Your staff, they comfort me.
You prepare a table before me in the presence of my enemies;
You have anointed my head with oil; My cup overflows.
**Surely goodness and lovingkindness will follow me all the
days of my life, and I will dwell in the house of the Lord forever.**"

TODAY'S SPECIAL

PSALM 23:6

117

THE PANTRY
LESSON 7

OVERVIEW

SPIRITUAL CONNECTION:

Pixel and Um's UPSIS makes national news. Even though it is time for Grandpa J to come home, he invites the kids to continue working at J's Diner for as long as they like. As they celebrate getting to stay at the diner, they are reminded of everything they learned from Psalm 23. Psalm 23 teaches that people who know Jesus will get to share His forever home of Heaven. That's a huge reason to celebrate!

CHARACTERS:

PIXEL - Tech savy, music loving, older brother of Um

UM - Talkative, story-telling, fun-loving, younger sister of Pixel

REPORTER SUSAN MOLASSES
Matter of fact reporter, always facing the audience as though on camera at all times

CAMERAMAN - Holds a camera on the reporter at all times, constantly changing camera angles (optional character who adds physical comedy to the reporter scenes)

COSTUMES:

PIXEL - Orange shirt, jeans, white apron, and diner hat

UM - Purple shirt, jeans, white apron, and diner hat

REPORTER SUSAN MOLASSES
Blazer, Collared shirt

CAMERAMAN - All black, headphones

PROPS:

- Banner: J's Diner Home of the UPSIS (Skit)
- Balloons (Skit)
- Various party supplies (Skit)
- Yarn (Bible Lesson)
- Clothes pins (Bible Lesson)

LEADER DEVOTION ● ● ● ● ●

READ PSALM 23, EPHESIANS 3:17-20, & REVELATION 21:1-8.

Psalm 23 follows a sheep and its good Shepherd through every season. In spring, the sheep enjoy the lush green pastures and quiet waters of the shepherd's home field. The good shepherd drives his flock to higher ground in the summer, facing many dangers on the way to the tablelands. Fall takes the flock to lower elevations. Finally, in winter, the shepherd takes his flock back home.

In every season of life, God is our Good Shepherd. He will guide us home to our final destination, home in Heaven. Home in Heaven! On earth, we sometimes fantasize about having bigger or better homes. What would it be like to live in the best house in the neighborhood, the White House, or Windsor Castle? Truthfully, none of those places could even compare to living in the home of the King of Kings! And though we may be able to visit bigger and better homes and enjoy them thoroughly, we are not invited to **visit** Heaven. We are invited to **stay**. We are invited to live in Heaven forever with the God who loves us so much.

As Christians, we are citizens of Heaven. We no longer belong to this world. We belong to the family of God, so goodness and lovingkindness should follow us everywhere we go. Because God has treated us with such grace, we are now called to treat others with the same.

Celebrate! Celebrate God's gracious love toward us, His sheep. Celebrate the fact of your final destination: Heaven. In every season, His children's destination is sure. We have hope in God's promise of Heaven. The troubles of this earth are only temporary, so give everything you have to Him. Stop spending time in worry and instead spend time in celebration, for you have a Good Shepherd who cares for your every need.

Celebrate the kids God has put in your group. Pray God will use you to introduce them to Jesus, the way to Heaven. Pray that even now, the kids will begin to understand the eternal significance of having a Heavenly Father, who invites them to live forever with Him in His heavenly home.

LESSON 7

PRE-SERVICE

Play a combination of upbeat music and fun video elements before worship begins. Encourage your JUMP Team to welcome kids and engage them in conversation.

COUNTDOWN VIDEO

JUMP Worship is starting! Lead the congregation in counting down. Worshiping together is fun, and we are ready to begin!

SONG

Lead the congregation in a fun worship song.

MAIN POINT VIDEO

WELCOME

Welcome to JUMP, where we worship God together! This is our last lesson in J's Diner. **SFX: SAD TROMBONE** But don't be sad yet. We are going to make this the best day EVER! We have learned so much from Psalm 23. The Lord is our Shepherd. He provides for us, guides us, protects us, corrects us, and has even prepared the way for us to live in Heaven with Him forever. Anyone who knows Jesus has a lot to celebrate! Our Main Point today is "The Lord Gives Me a Forever Home."

(Make motions to help kids understand the Main Point. Repeat the Main Point a few times together before continuing.)

Great job! Before we get started, we have a few rules to help us worship God together. Who remembers rule number one? Rule number one is STAY QUIET. God has something to say to you and me, and we do not want to miss it. Rule number two is KEEP YOUR HANDS AND FEET TO YOURSELF. Instead of using your hands and feet to bother people, use your hands and feet to worship God. Following this rule will help us focus on God and not on the people around us. Rule number three is STAND DURING SONGS. JUMP is not a show! When you hear a song, stand and worship with us. We want everyone to participate. The last rule is – say it with me - HAVE FUN!

We are going to have so much fun today at J's Diner! I can't wait to see if Pixel and Um will be able to save the diner. This really is going to be the best day EVER! Let's get started by talking to the Lord in prayer. Everyone bow your heads and close your eyes. We bow our heads to show respect, and we close our eyes to help us focus on God alone.

PRAY

Lead the congregation in prayer.

SONG

Lead the congregation in a fun worship song.

JUMP SKIT

See skit script beginning on page 124.

THE LORD IS MY
PROVIDER

LESSON 7 SKIT
THE LORD GIVES ME A FOREVER HOME

Skit Intro Video

UM: I can't believe it's already here!

PIXEL: What's already here, Um?

UM: The last day of work for us here at J's Diner. It's been AWESOME!!

PIXEL: It sure has! We have learned so much about working at the diner ... We even worked so hard we became managers!

UM: Plus, we created the Ummy Panini Sandwich ... Or the ...

UM & PIXEL: UPSIS

UM: And it's been a huge hit!

PIXEL: You know, we've learned a lot more than just how to run a diner and how to be a manager. We've learned how the Lord is our Shepherd.

UM: And how He's our Provider ...

PIXEL: Our Guide ...

UM: Our Protector ...

PIXEL: He's in charge ...

UM: He prepares a way for us ...

PIXEL: I'm so grateful the Lord has taught us all these lessons! I sure wish this wasn't our last day of work at J's Diner ...

UM: I wonder what Grandpa J wants us to do today?

Grandpa J Video 1

GRANDPA J: Well, hey hey hey! It's a great day with Grandpa J! It's so great to see your faces! I've got some GREAT news for you two!

UM: What is it Grandpa?

GRANDPA J: Your Ummy Panini Secret Ingredient Sandwich has made the national news! Everyone is talking about it!

PIXEL: What?!?!

GRANDPA J: You kiddos have made the national news! Everyone wants to try a bite of the famous UPSIS!

UM & PIXEL: NO WAY!

GRANDPA J: Yes way! Now, there is going to be a news reporter headed to the diner now! They want to interview you about the sandwich. They want to know how you came up with it and what inspired you to create it! I know you two have worked SO hard these past several days, so I want you to enjoy this time. Have a party! This is a BIG deal!

UM: AWESOME!

GRANDPA J: I'll see you two on TV!!! BYE!

Grandpa J Video 1 ends

PIXEL: This is the coolest day ever! Um, we've got to clean this place up to get it ready for all our guests!

SFX: SAD MUSIC

UM: Yeah, okay....

PIXEL: What's wrong, Um?

UM: Well, I just don't want to leave the Diner. I've loved all the time we've had together. I've loved getting to meet new customers and hearing their stories! I've loved that we created this sandwich together that everyone has heard about. I just don't want to leave...

PIXEL: I know Um. But right now, we've got to focus on celebrating all our hard work! Come on, let's get ready for our interview!

UM, PIXEL walk back on with REPORTER and CAMERA MAN.

REPORTER: So you two are siblings? Am I correct?

PIXEL: Yep! And proud of it! This is Um. Like the letters U and M. It's a nickname I came up with when we were little

UM: Because I'm always saying, "ummm this" and "ummm that."

REPORTER: Hahaha! *Overly cheesy news reporter laugh.* That is outstanding. Now tell me, this Ummy Panini Secret Ingredient Sandwich … Where did you get the inspiration for it?

UM: Ummm … Well, you see, Grandpa told us to create a new item for the menu. So, I created the Ummy Ultimate Sandwich and Pixel created the Perfect Panini Sandwich. And honestly, between you and me, they were pretty bad.

REPORTER: I see ….

UM: BUT THEN … We decided to combine our efforts and make the Ummy Panini Secret Ingredient Sandwich and it was AWESOME!!! *Both Pixel and Reporter cover their ears.* Oh, sorry!

REPORTER: You know kids, people are talking about this sandwich nationwide!

PIXEL: That's what we heard! We've started getting busier lately with customers coming by the diner to try it out!

UM: Yeah totally! People keep pulling off of Route 166 to come in here just for our sandwich! It's AWESOME!!! *Both Pixel and Reporter cover their ears.* Oh right … I'm sorry again. I just get a little excited!

REPORTER: Well, I can promise you one thing … As soon this news broadcast ends, you are going to have hundreds of new and eager customers walking through that door to try this UPSIS! Looks like you two have put J's Diner back on the map!

PIXEL: REALLY? You think we'll get new customers?

UM: So, we don't have to close the doors to the diner forever?!

REPORTER: Exactly!

UM and PIXEL start celebrating behind Reporter.

REPORTER: This is Susan Molasses reporting live from J's Diner. Back to you in the studio.

REPORTER: Thanks for taking the time to do an interview with us! Now I think you two need to throw a party! You're about to have a line that goes on for miles!

REPORTER and CAMERA MAN exit.

UM: Wow!! Let's get this place ready for a party!

PIXEL: And ready for customers!

Pull out balloons, a banner that says "J's Diner. Home of the UPSIS," and other various party supplies.

SFX: FUN MUSIC

PIXEL: Looks like the place is ready for customers. I just wish we could stay here to see and meet all these new people!

Grandpa J video 2

> **GRANDPA J:** Well, hey hey hey! It's a great day with Grandpa J! I just saw you two on the news! You looked great! I hope you are enjoying this moment! It's quite an accomplishment!

PIXEL: We are, Grandpa … We are so excited the diner is up and running again.

> **GRANDPA J:** Well, I've got some great news for you two. I want you to stay on and work at J's Diner for as long as you wish!

UM: REEEEALLY?

> **GRANDPA J:** Yes!

PIXEL: Is it because we've worked so hard to get new customers?

> **GRANDPA J:** Actually, no.

PIXEL & UM: It's not!?

GRANDPA J: No. you see Um and Pixel. You two are my family. You're my grandchildren. I love you with all my heart and I will always have a place for you at J's Diner. You two chose to work here this summer. You followed me here. And because you follow me, I will forever have a place for you. And you know kiddos, just like I will always have a place for you here at J's Diner, the Lord always has a home for us in Heaven, with Him. If we choose to follow Jesus, God will let us live in His home with Him! The Lord gives me a forever home. Can you all say that?

PIXEL & UM: The Lord gives me a forever home!

GRANDPA J: Exactly. And don't ever forget that! Now you two need to get back to celebrating! But this time, instead of celebrating the sandwich and the customers, I want you to celebrate the fact that we get to be in Heaven one day with God, Our Good Shepherd! Where His goodness and loving kindness will follow! That is something to celebrate! Love you and I'll see you soon! Bye!!

Grandpa J video 2 end.

PIXEL & UM: Bye!!!

UM: I can't believe we get to stay at the Diner for good!

PIXEL: Yeah, this is awesome! Now, let's get to celebrating!!

SFX: CELEBRATION MUSIC

Exit.

GAME VIDEO

SONG *Lead the congregation in a fun worship song.*

BIBLE LESSON

BIBLE LESSON INTRO VIDEO

 INTRO

Today we are going to talk about something absolutely amazing! We get to talk about the incredible place God has prepared for His children: we get to talk about Heaven!! As we have studied Psalm 23, we have learned about many of the amazing things that God does for His people. He is the Good Shepherd who provides for, guides, protects, corrects, and prepares the way for His sheep. He provides a home for His sheep that perfectly meets their needs.

 READ THE BIBLE

Read Psalm 23.

David is so excited he is a part of God's family! David is confident that he will get to live in Heaven with God forever. Heaven is God's forever home. God promises that everyone in His family will get to live with Him in Heaven forever.

It is important to know if you are a part of God's family. After all, what would you do if you went home with your family and saw a stranger on the couch? You might call the police! You know right away that person does NOT belong in your home! He is NOT a part of your family! But what if you went home with your family and saw your grandmother sitting on the couch? You would be excited! She is a part of your family. She belongs in your home with you.

In the same way, Heaven is God's home. Only the people in God's family get to live in God's home in Heaven. So how do you get to be in God's family? ADMIT you have sinned, or done wrong things. BELIEVE Jesus is God's perfect Son who chose to take the punishment you deserve when He died on the cross for the wrong things you have done. BELIEVE Jesus came back to life three days later! Then CHOOSE to put Jesus in charge of your life for forever. The Bible says that Jesus will forgive you for your sins, so you can live in Heaven with God. You can have a friendship with God!

OBJECT LESSON

MATERIALS: Yarn, Clothes pins

Now that you know how you can go to Heaven, let's talk about what Heaven will be like! Heaven is where God lives, so there is no need for a sun. God is Light! The streets are made of gold. The Bible says that God will wipe every tear from our eyes. There will be no more death or sickness or pain. There will be no more hurt feelings, because there will be no sin. We will finally be able to live the way God made us to live, in a perfect friendship with Him.

But really, we do not have to wait until Heaven to live the way God made us to live. We can start right now living with God and for God, saying no to sin and yes to Him.

Hold up a spool of yarn. Choose one JUMP Team Member to hold the end of a piece of yarn.

Let this yarn represent the timeline of someone's life. Let's say this is Bob's life. First, Bob was born.

Roll out a small piece of yarn, placing a clothespin on the yarn to represent Bob's birthday.

Bob took his first steps. His first word was "dada"!

Roll out a few more inches, placing a clothespin on the yarn to represent Bob's milestones. First steps, first words, etc.

Bob scraped his knee, learned how to swim, and made friends when he started his first day of school.

Roll out a few more inches, placing a clothespin on the yarn to represent these milestones.

One day, Bob decided to put Jesus in charge of His life. He asked Jesus to forgive him for his sins. Bob became a Christian and started his friendship with God.

Roll out a few more inches, placing a clothespin on the yarn to represent this date. Mark it in some way to indicate that this was his most important decision. Continue to roll out the yarn and mark it with clothespins as you illustrate the rest of Bob's life. You may need a few more volunteers to help you hold the string up.

Bob grew up. He went to high school and chose a great college. Bob got a job and had a beautiful family of his own. He lived to be a very old man. Because Bob had accepted Jesus as his Lord and Savior, Bob went to Heaven when he died.

Here's my question: when did Bob become a citizen of Heaven? At what point in his life did Bob belong in Heaven?

Walk back to the clothespin that represents the day Bob was saved.

Bob became a citizen of Heaven the moment that He chose to make Jesus his Lord and Savior.

Put the timeline down on the ground.

 ## APPLICATION

2 Peter 3:13-14 says, **"But in keeping with His promise, we are looking forward to a new heaven and a new earth. So then, friends, since you are looking forward to this, make every effort to be found spotless, blameless and at peace with Him."**

Because we know Heaven is coming for those of us who have accepted Jesus in our hearts, we should start living as citizens of Heaven today. Right now! Because of Jesus, we are already citizens of Heaven, so let's start acting like it! Goodness and mercy should follow us everywhere we go, because we know the God who is good and merciful.

Today's road sign says "Destination Ahead." As Christians, we know that Heaven is our final destination. No matter what happens here on earth, we know we have an eternity of goodness waiting for us in Heaven. So don't wait until you get to Heaven to start living as a citizen of Heaven! Start today! Celebrate the fact that Jesus has already prepared the perfect place for you to live by living for Him. Celebrate the amazing truth that you get to be a part of God's family by sharing God's goodness and mercy with everyone around you! God has given us a forever home in Heaven, and that is definitely something to celebrate!!!

PRAY

We are now going into our time of offering. "Offering" is a big word for present. This is the time when we give our presents to the Lord, our Shepherd. We give back to God from everything He has given to us. Let's stand together and sing this song as an offering, a big present to God.

THE LORD GIVES ME A FOREVER HOME

↑

DESTINATION AHEAD

OFFERING SONG

Lead the congregation in a slower worship song.

PRAY

Lead the congregation in prayer.

MEMORY VERSE VIDEO

MEMORY VERSE

Are you ready to finish memorizing Psalm 23? We are so close! First let's review what we have learned already. Remember, we sing the word "Psalm", because Psalms is a book of songs. (*Review the verses using the motions you used in the previous lessons.*)

Repeat after me:
Psaaaaalm 23. (*Psaaaaalm 23*)
The Lord is my shepherd. I shall not want. (*The Lord is my shepherd. I shall not want.*)
He makes me lie down in green pastures. (*He makes me lie down in green pastures.*)
He leads me beside quiet waters. (*He leads me beside quiet waters.*)
He guides me in the paths of righteousness (*He guides me in the paths of righteousness*)
For His name's sake. (*For His name's sake.*)
Even though I walk through the valley of the shadow of death, (*Even though I walk through the valley of the shadow of death,*)
I fear no evil, for You are with me. (*I fear no evil, for You are with me.*)
Your rod and Your staff, they comfort me. (*Your rod and Your staff, they comfort me.*)
You prepare a table before me (*You prepare a table before me*)
in the presence of my enemies; (*in the presence of my enemies;*)
You have anointed my head with oil; (*You have anointed my head with oil;*)
My cup overflows. (*My cup overflows.*)

Wow! Great job. The last verse in Psalm 23 says, "Surely goodness and lovingkindness will follow me all the days of my life, and I will dwell in the house of the Lord forever."

(*Ask kids to give suggestions for motions to the key phrases in the verse. Once you have decided on the motions, repeat verse 6 once together.*)

Repeat after me:
Surely goodness and lovingkindness *(Surely goodness and lovingkindness)*
will follow me *(will follow me)*
all the days of my life, *(all the days of my life,)*
and I will dwell in the house of the Lord *(and I will dwell in the house of the Lord)*
forever. *(forever.)*

Now let's put it all together! Let's say an entire chapter in the Bible together.
Ready, set, go!

Psaaaaalm 23. The Lord is my shepherd, I shall not want.
He makes me lie down in green pastures
He leads me beside quiet waters.
He restores my soul;
He guides me in paths of righteousness for His name's sake.
Even though I walk through the valley of the shadow of death,
I fear no evil, for You are with me;
Your rod and Your staff, they comfort me.
You prepare a table before me in the presence of my enemies;
You have anointed my head with oil; My cup overflows.
Surely goodness and lovingkindness
will follow me all the days of my life,
and I will dwell in the house of the Lord forever.

Great job! Now this is going to sound crazy, but do you think you can say an entire chapter of the Bible without any help? I think you can! Take a deep breath. Do a few stretches. Jump up and down three times. Are you ready? Let's do this in three, two, one! *(Remove the verse from the screens. Let kids lead you in reciting the verses. If possible, video the group saying the chapter from memory.)*

I'm so proud of you! Memorizing that many verses is not easy, but you did it.
Way to go!

SONG

Lead the congregation in a fun worship song.

ANNOUNCEMENTS

Use this time to encourage kids to bring friends and participate in whatever you may have coming up next.

REVIEW GAME

It's time for the REVIEW GAME!! I need one volunteer from each grade to come up on stage. I will choose people who have been listening and paying attention the whole service and want to play in our game.

Choose contestants and introduce them to the group in game show style.

During this game, your grade can win by getting very quiet when you hear the wrong answer and very loud when you hear the right answer. Each grade is going to have a different silly move and sound that you must do when you think you hear the right answer. *(Let your contestants choose a silly motion and sound for their grade.)*

I hope you are ready. I hope you have been paying attention, because the game begins ... NOW!

Give kids the opportunity to do their motions and silly sounds when they hear the correct answer. Award points to the grade who is the quietest when they hear the wrong answer and participates the most when they hear the right answer.

Question 1. What is our Main Point today?
    a. The Lord Gives Me a Home Just for Now.
    b. The Lord Gives Me a Forever Home.
    c. The Lord Gives Me Wheels of Chrome.
    d. Pixel and Um saved J's Diner.

Question 2. Where can you find today's Bible lesson?
    a. Mark 23
    b. Matthew 23
    c. Psalm 23
    d. Manhattan 23

Question 3. Who wrote Psalm 23?
    a. David
    b. Jonathon
    c. Peter
    d. A baby goat

Option: Find a short video clip of a baby goat screaming online. Play this short clip every time you use "baby goat" as a choice. Act surprised and confused every time it plays. Let the kids laugh, then repeat the question again.

Question 4: Psalm 23:6a says, "Surely _____ will follow me all the days of my life..."

    a. Pixel and Um   **c. goodness and lovingkindness**
    b. peanut butter and jelly   d. giant ice cream sundaes

Question 5: Psalm 23:6b says, "...and I will _____ the house of the Lord forever."

    a. look at   c. decorate
    b. sing about   **d. dwell in**

Question 6: Psalm 23:5a says, "You prepare a table before me in the presence of my _____."

    a. frienemies   c. sea anemones
    b. enemies   d. mommy

Question 7: Psalm 23:4a says, "Even though I walk through the valley of _____, I fear no evil, for You are with me."

    a. shenanigans   c. the shadow of wolves
    b. the shadow of baby goats   **d. the shadow of death**

SONG

Lead the congregation in a fun worship song.

DISMISSAL

KIDS

Reaching kids and their families for Christ by making programming for children Fun, Intentional, Scriptural, and Helpful.

I've never seen a curriculum that is both scripturally sound AND as fun as VBS! You've got to try it!

Karen M. | Children's Curriculum Developer

28nineteen™ can work with any church - whatever their size or their schedule.

Elizabeth W. | Children's Ministry Professional

"Go therefore and make disciples of all the nations, baptizing them in the name of the Father and the Son and the Holy Spirit, teaching them to observe all that I commanded you; and lo, I am with you always, even to the end of the age." Matthew 28:19-20

www.28nineteencurriculum.com

THE LORD IS MY SHEPHERD!

J's Diner is a seven week 50's diner-themed study on Psalm 23.
In Sunday School, kids learn the truth of Psalm 23 through fun activities,
engaging stories, and object lessons. In Children's Worship, skit
characters Pixel and Um run Grandpa J's diner in his absence.
Kids will laugh as they learn the lifelong truths in the Bible.
By the end of this fun-filled series, kids will not only memorize
Psalm 23, but also understand what each verse means.

ENJOY THE WHOLE SERIES!

www.28nineteencurriculum.com